D0118224

A BENCHMARK

The Golden Retriever

An Owner's Survival Guide

Maryle Malloy

Published by Doral Publishing, Phoenix, Arizona
Printed in the United States of America.

Edited by SageBrush Publications
Interior Design by The Printed Page
Cover Design by 1106 Design
Cover Illustration by Mia Lane

Library of Congress Card Number: 2003100549
ISBN: 0-944875-90-4

The product recommendations of the author are not considered to be an endorsement of any particular product or manufacturer by the publisher.

Acknowledgments

Those who have contributed to my education, training, and knowledge of the golden retriever breed throughout the years are legion. Because of them I have become a better owner, breeder, exhibitor, and human being. I offer my sincere thanks to the following people and organizations: to the members of the Rio Grande Golden Retriever Club of New Mexico for welcoming a "newbie." Jeanne Von Barby, your words of encouragement helped me stay the course with my first golden. Linda Atwell, your graciousness will always be remembered, and Betsy Stroll, thanks for believing in Trina from day one!

For Sylvia Donahey-Feeney and Bill Feeney, it is difficult to put into words what you mean to me. Without your support, advice, and love, I would not have realized my dream by half. Thank you for having the faith in my first breeding, for helping me find such outstanding homes, and for taking "Ruler" and "Hailey" and their offspring to the top. Thank you for your unwavering commitment to the breed through all the years. Thank you for the thousands of hours both of you have given as volunteers on various committees and boards that serve the interest of our breed. Thank you for always listening to my "off the wall" ideas and for great bottles of wine and gourmet meals. Sylvia, you're the "wind beneath my wings."

Thanks to the Evergreen Golden Retriever Club of Washington for the dedication and hard work of its members in producing hundreds of "golden" events and supporting puppy referral and rescue. The friendships and good times remain in my heart.

A huge hug for Debbie Kahla, my dear friend and traveling buddy. If we had a dime for every discussion we had on structure and movement in goldens, we'd be rich. Thanks for loving my dogs and sharing yours with me, for a shoulder to cry on, and for a strong word when I needed it. No two breeders ever came up with more dog names than Debbie and I!

Thank you to Linda Shea-Wolp, always kind, always cool, and the best obedience instructor I know. Linda, the life you gave our Torry was the best. You took him to heights I never dreamed of—OTCH, High In Trials, Gaines championships; you nursed him through cancer and gave him everything a golden deserves. I'm eternally grateful.

Kudos for dear Jo Simpson whose commitment to children and dogs provided the impetus for her to create a model program for a tough environment, the Echo Glen Youth Center. My hat is off to you for your years of service to 4-H and Junior handlers. Thanks also, Steve, for sharing your home and your favorite chair.

Thank you to Barbara Madrigrano for raising and showing Goodtimes dogs and for giving me the opportunity to have some of yours as well. You are not only beautiful but a kick in the pants! Most of all, thank you for giving my beloved "Mini" a great home. Thanks for supporting Nicole and "Mini" in Junior competition. Mini's BOB win at Westminster is one of my most cherished moments.

Thank you to the professional handlers who have made Goodtimes dogs and their offspring Champions, Group winners, Best in Show dogs, National and Regional Specialty winners, and Show Dog Hall of Fame members. In alphabetical order: Carol Boitano, Terry Boitano, Laurie Jordan, Pam and Al Sage, Randy Schepper, Bruce and Gretchen Schulz, Mike Stone, Erik Strickland, Amy Rodrigues, and Pam Tillotson.

Hey, to my southern friend Toni Norton. You're tiny, but your heart is huge, and your shoulders are broad! Thanks for so many laughs and keeping me in your heart. To Michele Stansbury for a little Rally daughter, giving Meg a wonderful home, great jokes, and reminding me during tough times that I would be ok.

Thanks to Roger and Kay Fuller for leasing me Dazzle and for a memorable National Field Trial (and fiftieth birthday!) Thank you, too, for helping me learn how to handle a hard driving, working retriever. The future of our breed is assured because of junior handlers, Carley and Cameron Simpson and Nicole Madrigrano. Traveling with you, mentoring you, and watching you outstrip me by a mile, has been a hoot. I have derived immense pleasure from watching each of you grow and blossom into beautiful, talented, and educated young women. Carley thank you for loving and showing Trina—she adores you. Nicole, thank you for being Mini's best friend.

To Harmon Rogers, DVM. All breeders cherish their veterinarian, but Harmon is much more than my veterinarian; he is my friend. Thanks for your sage advice, skilled hands, awesome mind, and huge heart and also to you and your family for giving "Oakley" a great life. Though we now live hundreds of miles apart, I think of you often.

I offer this small token of acknowledgment and a debt of gratitude to Marie Deyl. Your work in developing international golden retriever rescue and your support of people and ideas that benefit our breed is a little known fact. You are an inspiration to those who know and love you.

Thanks to all the individuals and families who have taken a Goodtimes puppy (or two) into their homes and hearts. The friendships we forged over the years have touched me deeply. Special thanks in this category go to: Pat and Mike Anderson, Valerie and Randy Anderson, Pam and Pete Starrett, and Wayne and Sue Carroll.

To Cannon Goodnight, my former husband and partner, thank you for always supporting my dream, for your love and care of all of our dogs, and for trusting me with the breeding decisions. There is no one I trust more in the whelping box than you. Godspeed.

Thank you Dr. Alvin Grossman, Doral Publishing, for the opportunity to write this book. Thanks also for many wins in the breed ring through the years.

To each of the contributing authors, Connie Cleveland, Kathryn Jones, Jackie Mertens, Chris Miele, Doug and Judy Spink, Ed and Marallyn Wight, and Jan Wall, thank you so much for your wonderful insight and instructions and for helping me write this book. It is true that the "sum of the parts is greater than the whole."

Last, but by no means least, thank you to my parents, for your faith in me. Even though the sport of dogs is not your thing, you have always been there, rooting me on—I love you! To my children and grandchildren, thank you for your love, support, and understanding—the future of my breeding program is in your hands.

This book is dedicated to

*The Golden Retriever Club of America
and all the volunteers, members, and breeders
past, present, and future who have worked
so diligently to preserve and protect the breed—
through education, research, rescue,
and sound breeding practices.*

Contents

FC/FTC/AFTCH Cedarpond Brasdor Skywalker   *Photo: Jackie Mertens*

Chapter 1
History of the Golden Retriever

These sections will provide you with valuable insight into why and how the breed came into being. They will explain what the term "sporting dog" means. If you're looking for a golden, they will help you determine if this is the breed for you. If you own a golden, they will provide you with greater insight into how and why he acts as he does.

▼ What History Tells Us About the Golden Retriever
▼ Why History Is Important

What History Tells Us About the Golden Retriever

In order to understand the physical, mental, and emotional traits of a particular breed of dog, one must understand the animals' history. The history of the golden retriever breed is a story that tells how and why the breed was originally developed, that is to say—the PURPOSE of the breed.

Today, when the vast majority of dogs are purchased as family pets, the history of a breed may seem unimportant. It is not! If you have chosen to own a golden retriever or are contemplating the purchase of a golden retriever, knowing the history and purpose of this breed will help you with understanding your dog's characteristics, training your golden, and living with the breed.

The golden retriever's history began in the British Isles during the nineteenth century. This was a time when the British "gentry"

1

was attempting to develop the perfect hunting dog. Prominent among this group was Sir Dudley Majoriebanks, later to become the first Lord Tweedmouth of England and Scotland. Sir Dudley Marjoriebanks, unlike many of his fellow dog breeders, maintained breeding records and recorded them in his "stud book." The most complete records of the development of the golden retriever are included in the record books kept from 1835 until about 1890 by the gamekeepers at Guisachan (pronounced Gooeesicun) at Inverness-Shire, Scotland, the estate of Lord Tweedmouth. This residence is now a historical monument visited by thousands of golden retriever fanciers from around the world.

In 1952, the original studbook of Lord Tweedmouth was made available by his descendants. An examination of these records revealed that Lord Tweedmouth developed a sophisticated method of line breeding, i.e., breeding related dogs with desired traits in order to improve those traits. Undoubtedly, the desired traits that Marjoriebanks sought were the friendly nature and disposition, the athletic ability, the love of water, and the natural instinct for hunting and retrieving for which golden retrievers are known.

What does his studbook tell us? In 1865, he purchased a yellow retriever named "Nous" from a cobbler in Brighton, England. The dog was given to the cobbler in exchange for payment of a debt. It was the only yellow pup in an unregistered litter of black wavy-coated retrievers. Marjoriebanks transported the dog to his home in Scotland where the dog adapted extremely well to hunting. Later, Marjoriebanks obtained a tweed water spaniel, which he named "Belle." He subsequently bred Belle to Nous, which produced four bitches that he named "Ada," "Primrose," "Crocus," and "Cowslip." Each of these females, particularly Cowslip, was bred. Cowslip was crossed with a tweed water spaniel resulting in offspring with a love of the water.

In Britain, early water dogs were commonly bred to land or field spaniels in order to develop water spaniels. The water spaniels were very intelligent, good swimmers, and were eager to please their masters. These water spaniels are credited with contributing to the temperament, intelligence, and retrieving skills of today's golden retriever. Majoriebanks maintained his breeding program with careful outcrosses to two black wavy-coated retrievers in order to improve the hunting retriever instincts. The wavy-coated retrievers that were used in Marjoriebanks breeding program are the ancestors of today's black flat-coated retrievers.

Eventually an Irish setter was bred to improve the upland hunting ability and to ensure desired color. Finally, a sandy-colored bloodhound was used to improve the tracking ability of the new breed. The studbooks reveal that the coat texture of these dogs varied from fox red, similar to the Irish setter, to cream, which is similar to the color of many British and Australian golden retrievers of today.

Flat-coats-golden were first registered by the Kennel Club of England in 1903. In 1911, the Golden Retriever Club of England was formed, and the Kennel Club of England recognized flat-coats-golden as a separate breed—yellow or golden retrievers. Several years later, the name yellow was dropped, and they became forever known as golden retrievers.

From England to America

The first documented golden retriever was imported to the United States in 1893. "Lady," as she was called, was owned by Archie Marjoriebanks, the youngest son of Lord Tweedmouth. The American Kennel Club (AKC) first registered a golden retriever in November 1925. However, it was not until the early 1930s that a serious interest in the breed developed. In 1933, Col. Samuel Magoffin's import, Speedwell Pluto, completed his American and Canadian Championships by winning Best in Show at Puget Sound, Washington. Speedwell Pluto was also the first golden retriever to win a "bench" or conformation title, completing his American Championship in November of 1932. Today, he is an honorary member of the Golden Retriever Club of America's Show Dog Hall of Fame.

In 1938, a group of dedicated owners in this country joined together to form the Golden Retriever Club of America (GRCA). Today the GRCA is the largest of all Parent Breed Clubs in the country with membership numbering more than six thousand! *Author's Note: Throughout this book the initials GRCA will be used as an abbreviation for Golden Retriever Club of America.*

Why History Is Important

Today golden retrievers are versatile, adaptable, and loyal companions. Their popularity as a breed has gained momentum through the years because they are loving, loyal, and beautiful. They are many things: the consummate family dog, a powerful hunting companion, a beautiful show dog, excellent in obedience, agility, and tracking competitions, marvelous guide and therapy partners, and highly regarded as search and rescue dogs. Very few breeds are as versatile as the golden retriever. For this reason, the golden retriever breed appears to have several distinct types with a variety of temperaments or personalities.

Reputable breeders spend time and money before choosing to breed a litter of puppies. A mating is determined because of the breeder's desire to capture various traits and abilities in order to achieve a specific result. This type of breeder does not breed to produce mass numbers of puppies to meet consumer demand. They breed to produce a puppy for themselves and others that will excel in the breeder's area of interest, be it field, obedience, the showring, etc. Because the golden retriever is so versatile, he or she often excels in several of these areas and is known as "an all-around dog."

There are golden retrievers who possess a tremendous drive and desire to hunt; there are those bred to achieve high scores in the Obedience and Agility ring; there are those bred with the hope of achieving status and recognition as champions in the showring. These are but a few of the areas of interest a breeder may choose to pursue. However, in every case, the golden retriever's sunny, warm, and loyal temperament, his willingness to please, and his tractability must be maintained. These features are of paramount importance. Whether you are choosing a puppy or already own a golden retriever, one of the keys to understanding your dog is knowledge about the pedigree or background of your dog, particularly the parents and grandparents of both the sire (father) and dam (mother). The breeder of your dog is best suited to provide you with this information.

Certificate of Pedigree

Sire: Ch. Ametlling's Buster Keaton (OS)
SE372357 (1-6-85) gldn
OFA GR 23478F24M
B: M. Burkz
O: W. Feeney
Group Winner

- **Sire:** Ch. Birnam Wood's Mountin' Ash (OS)
SD901349 (9-26-81) gldn
OFA GR 16012
Group Winner
  - **Sire:** Am-Can Ch. Kachina Twenty Karat (OS/SDHF)
OFA GR 11372
Best of Breed Specialty Winner
    - Ch. Gold-Rush's Great Teddy Bear (OS/SDHF) OFA GR 3779
      - Am-Bda Ch. Cummings' Gold-Rush Charlie (OS/SDHF)
      - Ch. Golden Pine Glory'bee's Angel (OD)
    - Am-Can Ch. Krishna's E Z Livin' (OD) OFA GR 4543
      - Ch. Autumn Lodge's Mister Zap CD** (OS)
      - Ch. Lark Mill Genevieve CD (OD)
  - **Dam:** Ch. Goldenloe's Cinnamon Sizzler (OD)
OFA GR 9984
    - Ch. Autumn Lodge's Mister Zap CD*** (OS) OFA GR 2600 Group Winner
      - Ch. Misty Morn's Sunset CD,TD,WC (OS/SDHF)
      - Autumn Lodge's L'il Indian
    - Ch. Gillnockie Vixen of Goldenloe CD (OD) OFA GR 3255
      - Ch. Misty Morn's Sunset CD,TD,WC (OS)
      - Ch. Goldenloe's Junior Miss (OD)
- **Dam:** Am-Can Ch. Amberac's Asterling Aruba (OD/SDHF)
SC823175 (8-8-79) gldn
OFA GR 11860
Best in Show Winner
  - **Sire:** Ch. Gold Coast Here Comes The Sun CD (OS/SDHF) OFA GR 7494
Best in Show Winner
    - Ch. Autumn Lodge's Mister Zap CD*** (OS) OFA GR 2600 Group Winner
      - Ch. Misty Morn's Sunset CD,TD,WC (OS/SDHF)
      - Autumn Lodge's L'il Indian
    - Mex CH. HGL Tomlin's Happy Together UD,WC OFA GR 5098
      - Am-Can-Mex Ch. Cal-Vo's Happy Ambassador CD (OS/SDHF)
      - Hammerlock's Ambrosia
  - **Dam:** Sunhaven's Amberac's Aruba (OD)
    - Am-Can CH. Krishna's Klassic Kachina (OS/SDHF) OFA GR 6493
      - Ch. Autumn Lodge's Mister Zap CD** (OS)
      - Ch. Lark Mill Genevieve CD (OD)
    - Can Ch. Goldacquest's Love Song CD OFA GR 7219
      - Ch. Misty Morn's Sunset CD,TD,WC (OS/SDHF)
      - Can Ch. Deogolsay's Amorous Aquolia CD (OD)

Dog Name:
Am-Can-Bda
Ch. Goodtimes Can't Stopthe Rain (OS)
SM991061/08 May 13, 1992 male
OFA GR 45607G25M
Best of Breed Specialty Winner
Group Winner

"Tank"

Dam: Ch. Quillmark's Spring Fling CD (OD)
SF589656 (5-21-89) gldn
OFA GR 35646G25F
B: M. Bennett
O: C. & M. Goodnight

- **Sire:** Am-Can Ch. Freedom's Celebration (OS)
SD317027 (6-11-81) gldn
OFA GR 15391
Canadian BIS Winner/Group Winner
  - **Sire:** Ch. Gold Coast Here Comes The Sun CD (OS/SDHF) OFA GR 7494
Best in Show Winner
    - Ch. Autumn Lodge's Mister Zap CD*** (OS) OFA GR 2600 Group Winner
      - Ch. Misty Morn's Sunset CD,TD,WC (OS/SDHF)
      - Autumn Lodge's L'il Indian
    - Mex CH. HGL Tomlin's Happy Together UD,WC OFA GR 5098
      - Am-Can-Mex Ch. Cal-Vo's Happy Ambassador CD (OS/SDHF)
      - Hammerlock's Ambrosia
  - **Dam:** Ch. Laurell's Xpectacious (OD) OFA GR 9169
    - Am-Can Ch. Goldrush's Contender UD (OS/SDHF) OFA GR 3643 BIS Winner
      - Ch. Misty Morn's Sunset CD,TD,WC (OS/SDHF)
      - Ch. Goldrush's Birch of Bearwood CD,WC (OD)
    - Ch. Little Bit of I'Lanell (OD) OFA GR 1755
      - Am-Can Ch. Laurell's Allspice CD (OS)
      - Hulls Bay Beauty
- **Dam:** Am-Can Ch. Mardovar's Goin' Magnum Mist CD (OD)
SE138214 (8-13-84) gldn
OFA GR 23531G29F
  - **Sire:** Am-Can Ch. Mardovar's Go Furr Broke (OS) OFA GR 19852G29M
    - Ch. Birnam Wood's Douglas Furr (OS) OFA GR 16014
      - Am-Can Ch. Kachina Twenty Karat (OS/SDHF)
      - Ch. Goldenloe's Cinnamon Sizzler (OD)
    - Goldrush's Southern Comfort (OD) OFA GR 13573
      - Ch. Goldrush's Judgement Day (OS)
      - Ch. Southern's Goldrush Flair CD (OD)
  - **Dam:** Mongold Bold Becky Mardovar CD,WC (OD) OFA GR 17264
    - Ch. Waverly Kyber King CDX,WC OFA GR 6890-T
      - Ch. Jungold Legend of Golden Pine (OS)
      - Lizanter Golden Days English import
    - Mongold Reckless Rebecca UD,WCX OFA GR 10922
      - Jungold's Gold-Rush Caleb CDX
      - Double J's Brynhilde CDX

I hereby certify that the above pedigree is true
and that all ancestors are of the same breed.

signed _____

Pedigree for Ch. Goodtimes Can't Stopthe Rain, OS

The Importance of Knowing YOUR Dog's History

If you are still searching for your golden, you have the opportunity to make certain that the type of dog you purchase comes from a "line" (parents, grandparents, etc.) whose temperament and aptitude match your lifestyle. If you already own a golden retriever, possessing this knowledge will help you to understand and train your dog so that he or she is a better companion. For example, if you are looking for a family pet who will play with the children, enjoy his daily walk, and relax next to your chair at night, you do not want to purchase a dog from a breeder who is concentrating on producing highly charged, hard-working hunting dogs. On the other side of that coin, if you're looking for a dog who "lives to hunt," will track through the fields all day, and willingly plunges into the water to retrieve your duck or bird, you do not want to purchase your dog from a breeder whose interests lie in producing quiet family dogs.

What Is a Pedigree?

A pedigree is a written document similar to a "family tree" or genealogy. It should contain at least three generations. That is to say, it will show the name of the dog, both the sire (father) and dam (mother) of the dog, grandparents, and great-grandparents. The sire's side of the pedigree is shown above the dog's name and is referred to as the "top line" of the pedigree. The dam's side of the pedigree is shown below the dog's name and is known as the "bottom line" of the pedigree.

Reputable breeders will always furnish you with a pedigree of the dog being sold and will also tell you why they chose to mate their female with the male. The reputable breeder's pedigree will most likely indicate that all the dogs in the pedigree have OFA numbers—indicating that the dogs in the pedigree are free of hip dysplasia. The dogs in the pedigree will most likely have AKC titles indicating that they have participated in conformation and/or performance events and have proven their worth as breeding stock.

The puppy mill or back yard breeder, on the other hand, will very rarely be able to provide a pedigree where all the dogs have health clearances and have competed in conformation and/or performance events to prove their temperament, structure, and

Certificate
of
Pedigree

Topbrass Pawsability *** Female
SN570467/08 Aug. 16,1998
OFA GR 69676E24F-T
OFA GR F1363F74F-I
Breeder: Topbrass Kennels
Owner: Jackie Mertens
2000 National Derby List

FC Windbreakers Premium Vintage, Can***
SN087102207 (6-30-93) gldn
OFA GR 50230E27M heart normal
CERF GR 15569/2000-04
B: W. & V. Swan
O: P. Danielo Malmgren
'95 High Pt. Derby Golden–28 pts.
99,'98 High Pt. Open Golden
Canadian Open Win

Topbrass New Lien On Life * (OD)**
SN058273/02 (12-9-97) gldn
OFA GR 47069G24F-T
CERF GR 13421J97-55
B: M. Maurer & K. Martin
O: J. Mertens
National Derby List

- **FC-AFC Mioak's Ruin Check (OS/FDHF)** gldn
  SE973462 (11-17-86) gldn
  OFA GR 30415G31M
  O: B. & B. Wilkinson
  National Derby List
  42 All-Age points
  - **Frisbie's Olympia Gold *** (OS)** OFA GR 22137 National Derby List
    - AFC Yankee's Smoke'N Red Devil (OS)/OFA GR 10127 sire of 7 FC/AFC
      - FC-AFC Northbreak Kinike Sir Jim (OS/FDHF) OFA GR 2961-T
      - Yankee Fluff **** OFA GR 4595
    - FC Windbreakers Razzmatazz (OD) OFA GR 10134 National Derby List
      - AFC Holway Barty (OS) OFA GR 1720
      - Nutmeg's Harvest Gold Heather ** OFA GR 6295
  - **Mioak's Golden Torch (OD)** OFA GR 18702
    - AFC Wild Fire of Riverview CDX, WCX (OS/FDHF)/OFA GR 6455 Dbl Hr Winner
      - Riverview Knike Rocket *** OFA GR 669
      - Riverview's Nestles CDX (OD) OFA GR 1692
    - Mioak's Ginger *** (OD) OFA GR 4858 National Derby List
      - AFC Holway Barty (OS) OFA GR 1720
      - Bonnie Brook's Mabel (OD) OFA GR 1991
- **Topbrass Tripp Of Deerwood (OD)** gldn
  SF198124 (11-14-85) gldn
  OFA GR 30796E45F
  CERF GR 11655J94-99
  B: J. & J. Mertens
  O: V. & W. Swan
  - **NAFC-FC Topbrass Cotton (OS/FDHF)** OFA GR 10152 all time high point FT Golden (274 pts) Double Header Winner! sire of 7 FC/AFC
    - AFC Holway Barty (OS) OFA GR 1720
      - Eng. FTCH. Holway Westhyde Zeus
      - Eng. FTCH. Holway Flush of Yeo
    - CH. Sunstream Gypsy of Topbrass (OD) OFA GR 3649
      - FC-AFC Tigathoe's Kiowa II (OS/FDHF) OFA GR 1832
      - Am-Can CH. Topbrass Topeka of Sunstream CD,WC (OD)OFA GR 2000
  - **FC-AFC Windbreaker Smok'N Zig Zag (OD/FDHF)** OFA GR 15275 84.5 all-age points
    - AFC Yankee's Smoke'N Red Devil (OS)OFA GR 10127 sire of 7 FC/AFC
      - FC-AFC Northbreak Kinike Sir Jim (OS/FDHF) OFA GR 2961-T
      - Yankee Fluff **** OFA GR 4595
    - FC Windbreakers Razzmatazz (OD) OFA GR 10134 National Derby List
      - AFC Holway Barty (OS) OFA GR 1720
      - Nutmeg's Harvest Gold Heather ** OFA GR 6295
- **Sky-Lab Argus of Belvedere***WPC (OS)**
  SC265574 (8-4-77) gldn
  OFA GR 8792
  B: T. Cornsill
  O: Mrs. M. Hitchcock
  All-Age pointed
  - **AFC Holway Barty (OS)** OFA GR 1720 CERF GR 1770/76-61 English Import sire of 8 FC/AFC
    - Eng. FTCH Holway Westhyde Zeus
      - Eng. FTCH Holway Zest
      - Westhyde Merry Lass
    - Eng. FTCH Holway Flush of Yeo
      - Eng. NFTCH Manorks of Wynford
      - Picture of Yeo
  - **Sky-Lab Gandy Dancer WCX (OD)** OFA GR 4916
    - Dual CH. & AFC Tigathoe's Funky Farquar (OS/FDHF) OFA GR 1877
      - FC-AFC-CFC Bonnie Brooks Elmer (OS/FDHF)
      - Tigathoe's Chicksaw*** (OD) OFA GR 258
    - AFC Bonnie Belle of Hunt Trails (OD/FDHF) OFA GR 3300
      - AFC-AFC Chief Sands (OS/FDHF)OFA GR 715
      - Bonnie Brook's Eloise WC OFA GR 2336
- **AFC Topbrass Comet (OD/FDHF)** gldn
  SE562463 (11-14-85) gldn
  OFA GR 26042G CERF GR 9147
  B: J. & J. Mertens
  O: M. Maurer & K. Martin
  - **NAFC-FC Topbrass Cotton (OS/FDHF)** OFA GR 10152 all time high point FT Golden (274 pts) Double Header Winner! sire of 7 FC/AFC
    - CH. Sunstream Gypsy of Topbrass (OD) OFA GR 3649
      - FC-AFC Tigathoe's Kiowa II (OS/FDHF) OFA GR 1832
      - Am-Can CH. Topbrass Topeka of Sunstream CD,WC (OD)OFA GR 2000
  - **FC-AFC Windbreaker Smok'N Zig Zag (OD/FDHF)** OFA GR 15275 84.5 all-age points
    - AFC Yankee's Smoke'N Red Devil (OS)OFA GR 10127 sire of 7 FC/AFC
      - FC-AFC Northbreak Kinike Sir Jim (OS/FDHF) OFA GR 4595
    - FC Windbreakers Razzmatazz (OD) OFA GR 10134 National Derby List
      - AFC Holway Barty (OS) OFA GR 1720
      - Nutmeg's Harvest Gold Heather ** OFA GR 6295

I hereby certify that the above pedigree is true and that all ancestors are of the same breed.

signed: _____

Pedigree for Topbrass Pawsability***

working ability. If you own a golden retriever and do not have its pedigree, you can order one from the American Kennel Club or Malcairn Pedigree Service. See the Appendix for details.

Chapter 2
Golden Retriever Breed Standard

▼ What Is a Breed Standard?
▼ Official Breed Standard for Golden Retrievers (AKC)
▼ Glossary of Terms
▼ Pictorial of Golden Retriever

What Is a Breed Standard?

All purebred dogs registered with the American Kennel Club have a breed standard. The breed standard is formulated and adopted by the "parent" club, in the case of the golden retriever, by the Golden Retriever Club of America. This breed standard is then approved by the AKC and adopted as the official breed standard for each registered breed of dog.

What Is the Purpose of Having a Breed Standard?

The purpose of a breed standard is to perpetuate and maintain the ideal dog as described in the standard. Reputable breeders use the golden retriever breed standard to evaluate conformation (structure) and retrieving instincts as they relate to the breed's purpose. For instance, a sporting breed is bred to hunt, so the structure and movement of the dog must support its ability to work in the field as a hunting dog. The breed standard is what AKC judges use as their "model" to evaluate and judge dogs in the conformation ring. The purpose of the conformation ring is to offer a venue for breeders to exhibit their breeding stock, to obtain a judge's evaluation, and to look at other breeders' stock. In recent years, showing dogs in the breed ring (dog shows) has also become a hobby and recreation for those purebred dog fanciers who simply enjoy showing their own dogs and experiencing the camaraderie found at the dog show. As you study the golden retriever breed standard, you will notice that it refers not only to structure, but to purpose. "Primarily a hunting dog, he should be shown in hard working condition…" In every aspect of the breed standard, the definitions align with and support the golden retriever's original purpose as a hunting dog. As you study the standard, keep in mind that the ENTIRE description of each component—head, bite, top line, forequarters, hindquarters, gait, condition, temperament, size, etc.—allows the golden retriever to do what he was originally created to do—retrieve, swim, run effortlessly, and be an honest, loyal hunting dog.

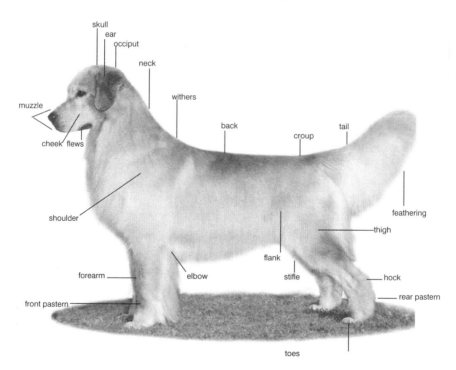

Golden with diagram of body parts

The Official Breed Standard of the Golden Retriever

General Appearance

A symmetrical, powerful, active dog, sound and well put together, not clumsy nor long in the leg, displaying a kindly expression and possessing a personality that is eager, alert, and self-confident. Primarily a hunting dog, he should be shown in hard working condition. Overall appearance, balance, gait, and purpose to be given more emphasis than any of his component parts.

Faults—Any departure from the described ideal shall be considered faulty to the degree to which it interferes with the breed's purpose or is contrary to breed character.

Size, Proportion, Substance

Males: 23-24 inches in height at withers; Females: 21½-22½ inches. Dogs up to one inch above or below standard size should be proportionately penalized. Deviation in height of more than one inch from the standard shall disqualify. Length from breastbone to point of buttocks slightly greater than height at withers in ratio of 12:11. Weight for dogs: 65-75 pounds; bitches: 55-65 pounds.

Head

Broad in skull, slightly arched laterally and longitudinally without prominence of frontal bones (forehead) or occipital bones. Stop well defined but not abrupt. Foreface deep and wide, nearly as long as skull. Muzzle straight in profile, blending smooth and strongly into skull; when viewed in profile or from above, slightly deeper and wider at stop than at tip. No heaviness in flews. Removal of whiskers is permitted but not preferred. Eyes friendly and intelligent in expression, medium large with dark, close-fitting rims, set well apart and reasonably deep in sockets. Color preferably dark brown; medium brown acceptable. Slant eyes and narrow, triangular eyes detract from correct expression and are to be faulted. No white or haw visible when looking straight ahead. Dogs showing evidence of functional abnormality of eyelids or eyelashes (such as, but not limited to, trichiasis, entropion, ectropion, or distichiasis) are to be excused from the ring. Ears rather short with front edge attached well behind and just above the eye and falling close to cheek. When pulled forward, tip of ear should just cover the eye. Low, hound-like ear set to be faulted. Nose black or brownish black, though fading to a lighter shade in cold weather not serious. Pink nose or one seriously lacking in pigmentation to be faulted. Teeth scissors bite, in which the outer side of the lower incisors touches the inner side of the upper incisors. Undershot or overshot bite is a disqualification. Misalignment of teeth (irregular placement of incisors) or a level bite (incisors meet each other edge to edge) is undesirable, but not to be confused with undershot or overshot. Full dentition. Obvious gaps are serious faults.

Neck, Topline, Body

Neck medium long, merging gradually into well laid back shoulders, giving sturdy, muscular appearance. No throatiness. Backline strong and level from withers to slightly sloping croup, whether standing or moving. Sloping backline, roach or sway back, flat or steep croup to be faulted. Body well balanced, short coupled, deep through the chest. Chest between forelegs at least as wide as a man's closed hand including thumb, with well developed forechest. Brisket extends to elbow. Ribs long and well sprung but not barrel shaped, extending well towards hindquarters. Loin short, muscular, wide, and deep, with very little tuck-up. Slab-sidedness, narrow chest, lack of depth in brisket, excessive tuck-up to be faulted. Tail well set on, thick, and muscular at the base, following the natural line of the croup. Tail bones extend to, but not below, the point of hock. Carried with merry action, level or with some moderate upward curve; never curled over back nor between legs.

Forequarters

Muscular, well coordinated with hindquarters, capable of free movement. Shoulder blades long and well laid back with upper tips fairly close together at withers. Upper arms appear about the same length as the blades, setting the elbows back beneath the upper tip of the blades, close to the ribs without looseness. Legs, viewed from the front, straight with good bone, but not to the point of coarseness. Pasterns short and strong, sloping slightly with no suggestion of weakness. Dewclaws on forelegs may be removed, but are normally left on. Feet medium size, round, compact, and well knuckled, with thick pads. Excess hair may be trimmed to show natural size and contour. Splayed or hare feet to be faulted.

Hindquarters

Broad and strongly muscled. Profile of croup slopes slightly; the pelvic bone slopes at a slightly greater angle (approximately thirty degrees from horizontal). In a natural stance, the femur joins the pelvis at approximately a ninety-degree angle; stifles well bent; hocks well let down with short, strong rear pasterns. Feet as in front. Legs straight when viewed from rear. Cow-hocks, spread hocks, and sickle hocks to be faulted.

Coat

Dense and water-repellent with good undercoat. Outer coat firm and resilient, neither coarse nor silky, lying close to body; may be straight or wavy. Untrimmed natural ruff; moderate feathering on back of forelegs and on underbody; heavier feathering on front of neck, back of thighs and underside of tail. Coat on head, paws, and front of legs is short and even. Excessive length, open coats, and limp, soft coats are very undesirable. Feet may be trimmed and stray hairs neatened, but the natural appearance of coat or outline should not be altered by cutting or clipping.

Color

Rich, lustrous golden of various shades. Feathering may be lighter than rest of coat. With the exception of graying or whitening of face or body due to age, any white marking, other than a few white hairs on the chest, should be penalized according to its extent. Allowable light shadings are not to be confused with white markings. Predominant body color which is either extremely pale or extremely dark is undesirable.

Gait

When trotting, gait is free, smooth, powerful, and well coordinated, showing good reach. Viewed from any position, legs turn neither in nor out, nor do feet cross or interfere with each other. As speed increases, feet tend to converge toward centerline of balance. It is recommended that dogs be shown on a loose lead to reflect true gait.

Temperament

Friendly, reliable, and trustworthy. Quarrelsomeness or hostility towards other dogs or people in normal situations, or an unwarranted show of timidity or nervousness, is not in keeping with golden retriever character. Such actions should be penalized according to their significance.

Disqualifications

Deviation in height of more than one inch from standard either way. Undershot or overshot bite.

Approved October 13, 1981
Reformatted August 18, 1990
Golden Retriever Club of America
American Kennel Club

Author's Note: The term disqualification in the breed standard refers to the fact that any dog or bitch shown in AKC breeding classes (conformation) that is over or under the standard by more than one inch or has a bite (tooth alignment) that is undershot or overshot will be disqualified by the judge and after three (3) such disqualifications may be barred from competition. Generally, dogs that have these disqualifications never make it to the showring, nor should they ever be bred.

Glossary of Terms Used in Golden Retriever Standard

Back | That part of the back line from the withers to the loin/croup junction; basically including the thoracic and lumbar vertebrae.

Balance | Refers to the symmetry of parts of the dog. It may refer to visual balance, e.g., the perception of symmetry of the various parts of the dog such as proportion, size of bone, relative length of parts such as neck, back, tail, etc. It may also refer to dynamic balance as in the symmetry of stride of front and rear assemblies and height to width as it influences movement (e.g., lateral motion).

Bone	The relative size of a dog's bone structure; substance.
Brisket	The formation of bone and muscle located at the base of the thorax or rib section between the forelegs; often referred to in describing chest depth.
Canines	The two upper and two lower fang-like teeth just outside the incisors.
Cat-Foot	A deep, round, compact foot where the two center toes are only slightly longer than the two outer toes; resembling a cat's paw.
Character	The expression, individuality, general behavior, and intelligence considered typical of a breed.
Chest	Generally, the part of the body known as the thorax; the part of the body enclosed by the rib cage. It may also indicate the front area of the dog's body at the terminus of the breastbone, sometimes referred to as the forechest.
Coming	As in "coming and going." Refers to the appearance of a dog's front assembly when he is "coming" toward the observer.
Conformation	The degree to which a dog conforms to the description of his breed in appearance, proportion, and structure as given in the standard.
Coupling	The coupling is the area encompassing the lumbar vertebrae and associated muscles of the loin and flank. It couples the front assembly to the rear assembly.
Covering Ground	An expression with a static and a dynamic application. When a dog is standing (static), it refers to the distance between the front and rear legs, i.e., synonymous with "standing over a lot of ground." When the dog is moving (dynamic), it means easy, efficient action with maximum reach and stride.
Croup	That part of the back line above the pelvis, from the loin section to the buttocks.

Dentition
Refers to the kind and number of teeth in the mouth.

Dew-claws
Vestigial or rudimentary toes, single or double, on the inside of the legs and above the feet. This growth would have been the big toe or thumb on a five-toed foot but has mutated to the present status. They are demanded on some breeds; not present or removed on others to avoid injury.

Diaphragm
A large muscular tissue separating the thorax or rib section from the abdomen, completely bisecting the body and functioning in the action of breathing.

Double Coat
Undercoat of soft, short, thick, close hair with longer, harsh hair growing through it to form outer coat or guard coat.

Open Coat
A coat lacking in undercoat or having guard hair that is too long or too fine and silky so that the coat lays too close to the body, giving an appearance of drooping.

Dudley
Nose that has a liver to flesh color. This coloration typically appears in the winter and is acceptable. Dog's who maintain this coloration year round lack sufficient pigment.

Elbow
The joint between the upper arm (humerus) and the forearm (radius and ulna); the point of the elbow being the tip of the ulna or the outer portion of the curve of this bone.

Feet
Consists of nails, toes, and pads. The golden retriever foot should be substantial, round, and compact, as in a "cat's foot."

Flank
The side of the body between the last rib and the hip.

Flat Croup
A croup with less downward inflection from the back line than is deemed suitable in the pattern of the breed in question; usually with less than thirty degree slope to the ground.

Forearm	The section of the front leg between the elbow and the pastern joint that is composed of the radius and ulna.
Foreface	That part of the head in front of the eyes; muzzle.
Forehand (forequarter)	The combined assemblies of the two front legs and the body that comes directly between them as we divide the dog into three sections: forehand, coupling, rear (hindquarters).
Front	The forepart of the body as viewed head-on, i.e., forelegs, chest, brisket, and shoulder line.
Gait	Any one of the various types of coordinated leg actions when the dog is moving; movement in the proper or designated manner. Gait is the term applied to the manner in which a dog progresses forward, i.e., walks, trots, or gallops.
Gaskin	Borrowed from horse terminology; that part of the hind leg between the stifle and hock joint, embracing the tibia and fibula. In the dog, this section of the leg is usually referred to as the second or lower thigh.
Gay Tail	A tail carried higher than perpendicular, up over the back.
Going	As in "coming and going." Refers to the appearance of the dog's rear assembly when he is "going" away from the observer.
Hip Joint	The ball and socket joint between thigh and pelvis.
Hock Joint	The assembly of tarsal bones in the back leg that make the joint at the lower end of the second thigh or gaskin and the hock (infrequently called the rear pastern) or metatarsus bones.
Hocks Well Let Down	A term that is synonymous with hock joint close to the ground; this produces a relatively short hock or cannon bone, which reduces the leverage applied by the Achilles tendon and lessens fatigue.

Incisors	The six upper and six lower front teeth, situated between the canines.
Jaws	The upper and lower part of the foreface or muzzle, the bones of which carry the teeth.
Knee	The stifle joint in the back leg between the first and second thigh, which is quite similar to the human knee with its cap.
Laid Back Shoulder	A shoulder blade inclined backward from the shoulder joint to the top of the blade at an efficient angle for the dog's work or action, forty-five degrees from the horizontal being the most efficient angle.
Legs	See limbs.
Limbs	The two front limbs consist of the shoulders, upper and lower legs, pasterns, and paws. The two rear limbs consist of the upper and lower thighs, hocks, and paws.
Loin	The section between the ribs and the croup, seven lumbar vertebrae and associated muscles.
Molars	The rearmost teeth in the dog's mouth; on each side there are two upper and three lower molars.
Occiput	The highest and rearmost point of the occipital crest in the center of the back edge of the skull; occipital protuberance.
Overshot	The incisors of the upper jaw striking ahead of and not touching those of the lower jaw; occurs to a variable degree.
Pads	Tough, thickened skin and connective tissue on bottoms of paws; soles.
Pants	The cluster of longer hair on the back of the rear legs; synonyms—breeches, furnishings, fringe.
Patella (Kneecap)	Held in place with strong tendons over the stifle (knee) joint, which is between the upper and lower thighs.

Pasterns	The metacarpal bones; the area of the foreleg between the pastern joint (carpus, wrist) and the foot.
Pelvis or Hip Bones	Ilium, ischium, pubes—these three bones meet to form the acetabulum, or the socket into which the upper end of the femur (upper thigh) fits to form a ball and socket joint. The foremost tip of the pelvis is felt along the spine at the tip of the croup, and the lower tip below the tail (pin or seat bones). The ischium also helps form the floor of the pelvis with the pubic bones, creating an aperture through which the internal organs make contact with the external.
Reach (or span)	Equal to one half the length of the stride, i.e., the distance between the tracks of the two front (or rear) paws.
Ribs	There are thirteen pairs of ribs. The first nine pairs are called true ribs and are attached directly to the sternum. The next three pairs are called false ribs and are attached to the sternum by means of a band of cartilage. The thirteenth pair does not attach to the sternum and is called floating ribs.
Ruff	Area of longer coat on the neck and shoulders surrounding the head.
Scissors Bite	When the cutting edges of the upper incisors strike slightly in advance of those in the lower jaw, passing them by with faces still touching, as do the blades of scissors.
Shoulder Blade (Scapula)	A flat, somewhat triangular bone with a ridge approximately on its centerline; the uppermost bone of the column of bones making up the front limb.
Spring of Ribs	The gradual slope and curvature of the ribs from their attachment to the vertebrae, creating a pronounced arch that increases the space for the heart and lungs.

Snipy Face	A slender tapering face, lacking fill-in before the eyes and bone foundation above the teeth of the upper jaw; over-refined, pointed muzzle.
Sternum (Breastbone)	The bones and cartilage that form the floor of the chest.
Stifle Joint	The joint between the upper and second thigh in the back leg.
Stop	A stepdown in the topline from the skull to the muzzle in the area between the eyes.
Stride	The distance between successive paw prints of the same limb. The length of stride increases with speed up to the maximum determined by the animal's structure.
Top Line	The line or profile of the dog from neck to base of tail, including wither, back, loin, and croup.
Track	The pattern made by the paw prints as the dog gaits.
Trot	Most commonly used gait; it is the dog's long distance type of locomotion. The dog is supported by two diagonal limbs, either the right front and the left rear or the left front and the right rear.
Type	A word encompassing the characteristic qualities distinguishing a breed; the embodiment of a standard's essentials. A dog with type has those characteristics that make it the best type for its purpose. Those characteristics for the golden retriever usually include, among others, size and proportion, appearance, coat, movement, and temperament.
Undercoat	In double-coated breeds, the undercoat is short, soft, and dense supporting the guard hair and acting as a weatherproof, insulating blanket.
Undershot	The lower incisors jut out in front of the uppers.

Vertebrae   The bones composing the spinal column. From head to tail, they run, seven cervical of the neck, thirteen thoracic of the chest, seven lumbar of the loin, three fused sacral in the croup, and five to twenty-two coccygeal of the tail.

Walk   The slow form of locomotion. The dog moves forward one limb at a time, and his body is supported by two or three limbs at all times. In this gait, the rear tracks never reach the front tracks, and the legs only converge slightly toward the midline of the body.

Withers   The region of the top of the shoulder blade and the first and second thoracic vertebrae. The withers are located just behind the neck at the neck/back junction. The withers are considered the highest point of the back and are used to measure the height of the dog.

Chapter 3
Golden Retriever Health Issues

One of my objectives in writing this book is to provide clear, concise, and up-to-date information on the golden retriever breed. This book would not be complete without a description of the most common diseases affecting the golden retriever breed.

There are four diseases for which reputable breeders screen: hip and elbow dysplasia, cataracts, and heart disease. There are others that affect the breed, for which no proven screening method is available. They have been listed here as well. When you see the term Health Clearance, it refers to the clearance document obtained from a recognized health registry and/or Board Certified Veterinarian.

▼ Health Clearances
▼ Hereditary Problems

Health Clearances

When I refer to health clearances, I'm referring to those clearances that should be obtained on any sire and dam prior to breeding. Members in good standing with the Golden Retriever Club of America always obtain these health clearances. These members adhere to the GRCA Code of Ethics. They obtain the clearances from the following organizations: OFA, PennHip, Board Certified Veterinary Ophthalmologists (CERF), and Board Certified Cardiologists.

All AKC breeds have a parent club or national organization with rules and regulations and a code of ethics. The AKC is a registry for purebred dogs in the United States. The organization does not "police" breeders to make sure they have obtained health clearances. No one "polices" breeders. The most that you can hope for is to purchase your puppy from a reputable breeder who subscribes to the GRCA Code of Ethics.

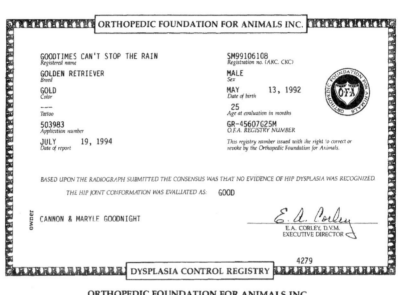

OFA Hip and Elbow Certificates

Hereditary Problems

The vast majority of golden retrievers can live long healthy lives if given a high quality diet, regular exercise, water, fresh air, routine veterinary care, and love. Nevertheless any dog can fall victim to a wide range of acquired health problems.

Each breed of dog has hereditary problems. Problems that affect one or more breeds may be nonexistent in others. Some of the hereditary problems may have a tendency to "run in families" while others may be seen with less frequency. The golden retriever is NO exception, and as the popularity of the breed increased, unfortunately the problems multiplied. Why? Because of the demand, there are those who, for a profit, breed indiscriminately. Failure to screen for hereditary problems before the breeding takes place often results in the "doubling up" of unfavorable genes, and the results are distressing for the buyer and the dog alike. It is also important to recognize that even with consistent screening and health clearances for both sire and dam, no breeder can guarantee that every puppy in a litter will be free from hereditary defects.

Hip Dysplasia[1]

The term hip dysplasia means poor formation of the hip joint and describes a developmental disease in young dogs of many breeds. Unsound hip joints are a common problem in the larger breeds and can be a serious problem for any dog that is to be trained for a demanding activity such as field/hunting, agility, tracking, or search and rescue.

Hip dysplasia is an inherited defect. However, the expression of this genetic defect can be modified by environmental factors such as over nutrition (a fat puppy plus rapid growth is a formula for disaster), excessively rapid growth (feeding a high-protein, high-fat diet that stimulates rapid growth), and certain traumas during the growth period of the skeleton. As with any quantitative trait, hip

---

1   Indicates basic health clearances that should be
     obtained on all breeding stock prior to being bred.

joint conformation can range from good to bad with all degrees in between. Signs of hip dysplasia cannot be detected in the new-born puppy, but usually appear in the rapid growth period between four and nine months of age. Signs of the disease can vary widely from slight irregularities of gait to crippling lameness. Improvement or even apparent disappearance of lameness can occur as the dog matures, as a result of the joint stabilizing, inflammation subsiding, and musculature strengthening. However, the dysplastic dog will usually develop some degree of arthritis later in life.

If your dog appears lame for more than a day or two and you know he did not injure himself some other way, you should take him to your veterinarian for an examination. He will probably need to do a radiographic examination (x-ray) to determine the cause of the pain. The dysplastic dog should not be used for breeding, but may well lead a long, happy, and useful life. During the acute phase of the disease, your veterinarian may suggest rest and supportive care. Moderate and regular exercise, control of weight, and anti-inflammatory drugs are helpful in managing arthritis associated with hip dysplasia in an older dog. Many goldens with hip dysplasia show no outward signs at all until they are seven to eight years of age when muscle tone decreases and arthritis becomes apparent.

Elbow Dysplasia[2]

Elbow dysplasia is the term for an elbow joint that appears malformed on x-rays. The mechanism of the malformation is unclear, but it may be due to differences in the growth rates of the three bones that make up the elbow joint. In mildly affected dogs, the only consequence may be arthritis. In more severely affected dogs, osteochondritis dissecans (OCD) can result from the stress in the joint. These changes are visible on x-rays; the Orthopedic Foundation for Animals (OFA) evaluates the x-rays for evidence of elbow dysplasia.

---

2   Indicates basic health clearances that should be obtained on all breeding stock prior to being bred.

Due to the number of possible complications, it is hard to make predictions about how elbow dysplasia will affect a dog. If it can be identified at a young age before changes are severe, surgical correction has a reasonably good success rate. Once severe changes set in, it is much harder to prevent subsequent arthritic changes. Most dogs with this condition eventually become lame, and the lameness can be very severe, even to the point of disuse of one leg or severe difficulty getting up and walking even short distances.

Treatment consists of surgical correction of whatever complications are present, if possible. Medical management using aspirin or other anti-inflammatory medications is helpful. Weight control is very important over the long term for success of either surgical or medical management of this condition.

Correct Positioning for OFA Radiographs

Not every veterinarian is skilled at positioning a dog for OFA or PennHip films. If you are attempting to get a clear concise rating from these organizations, it is imperative that you submit an x-ray that truly depicts the condition of your dog's hips and/or elbows. Before selecting a veterinarian for this procedure, check with your breeder for a recommendation. All reputable breeders know veterinarians in their area who are proficient in positioning. Your x-rays should be sent to either the Orthopedic Foundation for Animals (OFA) or to Synbiotics (PennHIP) for diagnostic evaluation. While the two evaluation procedures differ somewhat, GRCA recognizes the validity of both and encourages all breeders of golden retrievers to determine the conformation health of the hips for any potential breeding animal.

Authors Procedure for Evaluating Hips and Elbows

At one year of age I do what I call "look see" radiographs. That means I'm looking for a base line to see if there is any evident problem. I don't use anesthesia unless my dog won't relax. If either hip or elbow radiographs indicate a problem, I get a second opinion (generally from a Board Certified Veterinary Radiologist.) Should the diagnosis be confirmed via the second opinion, I spay/neuter the dog and place the dog in a family home with full disclosure. If the dog looks good at one year of age, I radiograph again when the dog is two years of age. At this point I plan to send the radiograph to OFA for an evaluation. See caution on bitches in season.

Here is a description of the procedure I follow when doing radiographs for submission to the OFA.

1. I always have my radiographs taken while the dog is under anesthesia. I wait while the radiographs are being taken.

2. When the radiographs have been developed, I review them with my veterinarian. We discuss the positioning and his evaluation. If there is a question on positioning, we do another radiograph and evaluate it and compare it with the first. We select the best one, and if all looks good, he submits it to OFA for evaluation.

3. If for some reason we question the radiograph or it clearly looks like the dog has a problem in either hip or elbow, we send it to the Board Certified Veterinary Radiologist.

4. Pending the outcome and diagnosis by the Board Certified Radiologist, I do one of three things: a) submit the radiograph to OFA for an evaluation, b) take additional radiographs to try to get better positioning so I am submitting the best radiograph of the hips/elbows possible, c) if a problem is confirmed, I spay/neuter the dog and place it in a family home with full disclosure.

Caution: Do not radiograph your bitch within sixty days of her estrus cycle (sixty days before her cycle or after cycle). The hormones in her system can affect the joint laxity and may give you a false reading.

Eye Disease³

Hereditary cataracts are a common eye problem in golden retrievers. A "cataract" is defined as any opacity within the lens of the eye. At least one type of hereditary cataract appears at an early age in affected golden retrievers. This type of cataract is referred to as a "juvenile cataract." While cataracts may or may not interfere with the dog's vision, some types do progress into severe or total loss of vision.

Non-hereditary cataracts can sometimes occur, and examination by a Board Certified Veterinary Ophthalmologist is necessary to determine if the cataract is or is not of concern from a genetic standpoint. If there is any question, the dog is certainly not to be recommended for breeding. A few families of golden retrievers carry genes for Central Progressive Retinal Atrophy, commonly referred to as CPRA. CPRA is a progressive deterioration of the light-receptive area (retina) of the eye and may result in complete blindness at a fairly young age. There are also other eye defects, such as retinal dysplasia, that prevent consideration of a dog as a breeding animal. Eyelid and eyelash problems also may occur in the breed; some have a hereditary basis, and some are due to other factors. Entropion and Ectropion is the turning in or turning out of the eyelids. Trichiasis and Distichiasis involve eyelashes or hairs rubbing on and irritating the eye. Surgery may be needed to correct these problems, and while it is a fairly simple procedure, such dogs should not be bred and are ineligible to be shown under AKC rules.

Eye examination of breeding stock should be done ANNUALLY, until at least eight years of age and preferably longer, as hereditary eye problems can develop at varying ages. All eye examinations are to be made by a Board Certified Veterinary Ophthalmologist who has the special equipment and training needed to properly examine the dog's eyes.

Dogs that have been thus examined and found to be free of hereditary eye disease can be registered with the Canine Eye

---

3   Indicates basic health clearances that should be
     obtained on all breeding stock prior to being bred.

Registration Foundation (CERF). CERF assigns the dog a number which, when properly understood, helps to make eye clearances more meaningful. For example, CERF GR 1857/89-102 means that this dog was the 1,857th golden retriever to be registered with CERF; that the most recent examination indicating this dog free of hereditary eye disease was done in 1989; and that the dog was 102 months old at the time of the examination. Dogs with hereditary eye disease should not be used for breeding.

Heart Disease[4]

The most common hereditary heart disease found in golden retrievers is subvalvular aortic stenosis, commonly referred to as SAS. Every prospective breeding animal should be examined by a Board Certified Veterinary Cardiologist. If a murmur is detected through auscultation (listening with a stethoscope), additional diagnostic tests may be recommended. However, even if the results are negative, this does not rule out heart disease, as some mild but hereditary forms may be undetectable except on necropsy. Dogs with hereditary heart disease should not be used for breeding.

There are additional topics such as hypothyroidism, seizure disorders, and other orthopedic disorders for which routine screening of golden retrievers is not performed. This may be because acceptable examination standards have not yet been developed or because the incidence of the defect is low in the golden retriever breed. Potential buyers should feel free to ask the breeder about these or any subjects of concern to them. The exchange of such information is an expected and customary practice. Following are a few more problems that seem to occur more frequently in the golden retriever breed.

---

4   Indicates basic health clearances that should be
     obtained on all breeding stock prior to being bred.

Megaesophagus

This is a condition in which the esophageal muscles lose their strength and the esophagus dilates to a much larger size. Usually dogs with this condition regurgitate food as well as water. Sometimes the enlarged esophagus is visible on plain x-rays of the chest, but often it is necessary to use some kind of contrast medium like barium to make the enlargement visible.

Panosteitis

Panosteitis is a spontaneously occurring lameness that usually occurs in large breed dogs. German shepherds seem to be particularly predisposed to this condition. (*Author's note: Certain lines of golden retrievers are also predisposed to this condition.*) Due to this, it is possible that the disease may have genetic causes. Some veterinarians feel that this disease may be induced or worsened by stress. Affected dogs are usually in the five to fourteen month age range, but can occur in dogs as young as two months. Male dogs are more commonly affected than female dogs.

The lameness tends to occur very suddenly, usually without a history of trauma or excessive exercise. In most cases, one of the front legs is affected first, and then the problem tends to move around, making it appear that the lameness is shifting from leg to leg. There are often periods of improvement, followed by worsening of the symptoms in a cyclic manner. This makes evaluation of treatment difficult, since many dogs will spontaneously recover with or without treatment and then relapse.

X-rays usually reveal that the bones have greater density than is normally found. If pressure is applied over the long bones, pain is usually present. The x-ray signs do not always match the clinical signs. In most cases, the worst pain lasts between one and two months but may persist in a cyclic nature for up to a year. Analgesic medications like aspirin can be helpful. In severe cases, corticosteroids may provide relief. A common rumor is that low-protein, low-calcium diets may prevent this condition. It should be noted that the energy level of low-protein/calcium diets is often lower as well. If this is the case, a puppy will eat much more of the diet in order to meet its energy needs, resulting in higher total calcium consumption. It may be preferable to feed a large breed puppy diet and restrict total quantity to keep the dog lean than to use a low-protein/low-calcium adult dog food. See Chapter 8, "Maintaining Your Golden Retriever's Health." This condition is self limiting, meaning that it will eventually go away, with or without treatment. Pain control can go a long way towards helping your pet feel more comfortable and should be used.

Cancer

Cancer is the term for several diseases all characterized by unregulated cell growth. Cancers can be further described by the type of cell in which the abnormal growth originated: osteo (bone), lympho (lymphocytes or white blood cells), hemangio (blood vessels), mammary (breast). Thus the terms: osteosarcoma, lymphoma, hemangiosarcoma. The two types of cancer most often found in goldens are hemangiosarcoma and lymphosarcoma. Cancer is a growing problem for all breeds. Current studies indicate that approximately sixty percent of all deaths in the golden retriever breed are caused by cancer. The great majority of these deaths occur in dogs age 10½ to 12, however there are still many instances where cancer takes the life of a dog in its prime.

The Golden Retriever Club of America is working vigorously with other breeds and research organizations and has committed thousands of dollars for research. For up to date information, log onto the GRCA's web site: www.grca.org.

Chapter 4

Finding Your Golden Retriever

Finally! We're ready for the fun part, finding your dog. For all you readers who already own a golden, I hope you'll read these pages as well. Perhaps you have a friend or relative who is looking for a golden retriever and you can pass this information along. Your knowledge will impress them and could make a big difference in the life of a golden.

▼ Do Your Homework
▼ Choosing a Reputable Breeder
▼ Puppy Mills/Pet Shops
▼ The Back Yard Breeder
▼ The Serious Hobby Breeder
▼ What to Expect from a Breeder
▼ How Much Does a Golden Cost?
▼ Male or Female, Does It Matter?
▼ Selecting Your Puppy
▼ Consider the Older Dog
▼ GRCA Puppy Referral

A litter of beautiful Birnam Wood puppies   Photo: Julie Schepper

Do Your Homework

Before you start looking at litters of puppies, take time to learn about the breed. Reading this book is a start. Now, attend dog shows, field trials, hunting tests, obedience, and agility trials. To find the date, time, and location for these events, go to the web site: www.akc.org. In the events section, you can find every event in your area. Attend a meeting of your local golden retriever club. To find a club near you, visit the web site: www.grca.org. Talk with owners and breeders at these events. They are proud of their dogs and happy to share their enthusiasm.

Choosing a Reputable Breeder

Look around. It is much easier to find a "puppy mill" or "backyard breeder" that knows and cares little about the welfare of the breed than it is to find a reputable breeder. Have patience, and never buy impulsively; all puppies are cute! The Golden Retriever Club of America and many of its local member clubs (see Appendix) can supply you with a list of conscientious breeders in your area who will help you in your search, even though they may not have anything for sale themselves.

Approaching Owners and Breeders During a Competition

Dogs being prepared for competition are athletes. Their owner/handlers are focused and should not be disturbed while preparing to perform. If you approach them during this time, they may be brief and tell you "this is not the time to talk to me." Be observant; if you are at a dog show wandering about the grooming area and see a dog you like, ask the person if he or she has time to speak with you. Stand outside the showring; observe the dogs and their handlers. When you see a dog that "strikes your fancy," note who the handler is, and when he or she is finished competing, ask if he or she has time to talk to you. Follow this procedure at any competitive event, and you will find people who will take the time to speak with you or at least give you information on how you can contact them to schedule a visit and meet their dogs.

Contacting a Breeder

Be persistent. Reputable breeders are often inundated with calls and emails. A breeder who has no puppies on the ground and is not planning a litter in the very near future is by necessity reluctant to return long-distance calls. If you are calling breeders and reach an answering machine, be sure to leave the message that they may call you back—collect. This will generally assure you a return call, and often that breeder will be able to refer you to another reputable breeder who has just what you are looking for.

Sample Phone Message: Here is a script of the ideal telephone request from a person looking for a puppy.

> *"Hi, my name is _____, and I'm looking for a golden retriever (puppy), (older dog). I live in _____, and my wife (or husband) and I have __ children ages _____. We would like to talk with you about your dogs and set up a time to visit. If this is a long distance call, please feel free to call us back collect or email us at _____."*

You get the idea. Whether you're a single person or married, with or without children, the point is, you are telling the breeder that you are seriously interested in acquiring a golden.

Emailing a Breeder

When you send an email inquiry to a breeder, be sure to include the same information you would give him or her if you were leaving a phone message. Nothing is more frustrating to a breeder than to receive an email that says, "Do you have any puppies?" The majority of breeders will simply hit the delete button. A breeder wants to know to whom he or she is writing. Remember, the breeder may not have puppies available, hasn't heard your voice, doesn't know whether you are sincere, and probably receives a lot of email and phone call inquiries. Replying to such inquiries takes energy, time, and money. So, if you want to connect with a reputable breeder or have a breeder provide you with a referral, you must give him or her a reason to want to reply to your request for information.

Pet Shops and Dealers

CAUTION: Purchasing your puppy from a pet shop or dealer is the worst possible choice! The puppies are poorly bred and raised. They are thought of as merchandise to be sold for a high profit. The high profit results because little has been put into the breeding or the care of the puppies. Many are sickly. The dealer breeds his dogs from a very young age, litter after litter. Their poor bitches are often kept in small confined spaces with no socialization. To puppy mill breeders, puppies are a commodity! Dealers sell their puppies to pet shops. When you give your money to this type of breeder or pet shop, you are perpetuating the problem that reputable breeders everywhere are fighting against.

The Back-Yard Breeder

The back-yard breeder is also a poor choice. This is the person who owns a pet golden and thinks it would be "fun" to have puppies, that it would be a great experience for the children, or that the bitch "should be bred once before she is spayed." Even worse, in some cases, it's done just to make money. Usually this breeder knows little about the standard or history of the breed and still less about proper care. The back-yard breeder is not aware of breed problems and doesn't take the time to learn. This person's only goal is to produce puppies, and when the "fun" is over, to sell them quickly. The ads you see in your local paper for golden retriever puppies are generally placed there by puppy mill breeders, dealers or back-yard breeders.

The Serious Hobby Breeder

The serious hobby breeder is your very best choice for purchasing a puppy. The serious and dedicated hobby breeder regards his or her dogs as even more than a hobby; they are a passion. This type of breeder is involved in dogs for the enjoyment of each individual animal, participates in one or more aspects of the "dog sport," and is interested in producing the finest animals possible. Therefore, the results are superior. The best breeders acknowledge responsibility for each and every puppy produced and stand behind every dog they have bred. Unequivocally, your choice should be from the ranks of the serious hobby breeder. It is an interesting fact that poor quality puppies from pet shops and back-yard breeders are often sold for the same price and sometimes even more than those purchased from the experienced hobby breeder. The question is, how does one recognize the responsible breeder? The following page lists requirements the breeder should meet before you consider purchasing a puppy. Don't be afraid to confront the breeder with these requirements. It is your right, and you can rest assured that the dedicated breeder will respond to your questions positively and with pride. (See Appendix for GRCA and local club breeder referrals.)

The Anderson Family—Hard work and dedication are the hallmarks of a reputable breeder.   *Photo: Maryle Malloy*

What Constitutes a Serious Hobby Breeder?

The serious hobby breeder is:

1. A member in good standing of the Golden Retriever Club of America.

2. A member in good standing of a local Golden Retriever Club or an All-Breed Club. Ideally he or she should belong to all three, however, sometimes that is impossible due to location and/or time commitments. This type of participation indicates "depth" of involvement. This breeder is exposed to other points of view, learns more about the breed and modern breeding practices, and is knowledgeable about the AKC Rules and Regulations regarding Registration and Performance Events.

3. This breeder is involved in showing his or her dogs in the breed ring, the obedience ring, hunting tests/field trials, agility, tracking, or a combination of any of these areas. Such participation indicates that the breeder is not working in a "vacuum." If a breeder does not participate in these activities, he or she really has no idea how good (or

bad) his or her dogs are. The breeder is deprived of the opportunity to share information and ideas with others. Showing provides the competition that encourages breeders to produce better dogs. They are able to visually compare their dogs with others and to see other dogs that they may wish to include in future breeding plans. The breeder who competes wants to prove how good his or her dogs are and is putting his or her breeding program "on the line." This breeder is not relying on just a pedigree to indicate quality. Even if you do not want a competition animal, you deserve a companion that is the end result of a carefully planned litter, a puppy that received the same care as the potential champion. The breeder who competes in organized activities is known by others and has a reputation to uphold. This breeder will be as careful and honest in selling you your pet puppy as in selling show stock.

4. The breeder will be able to show you a clean environment, healthy, well-socialized puppies, and a dam with a good temperament. The stud dog (sire) will usually belong to another breeder and may not live locally. If he does, you may also wish to visit his owner to look at his structure and evaluate his temperament.

What To Expect From A Breeder

You should expect:

▼ The breeder to give you a period of time to have the puppy examined by a veterinarian to determine its state of health, so that both of you are assured about the condition of the puppy at the time of sale. If a problem should arise, it can then be quickly resolved.

▼ Along with feeding instructions, the breeder should provide you with a record of the dates and types of de-worming, vaccinations (if any), a three-to-five-generation pedigree, and a form to register the puppy with the American Kennel Club (AKC). Sometimes the registration form is not available, and in that event, you should receive a written

Madelyn Knight and Top Brass puppies

Photo: Jackie Mertens

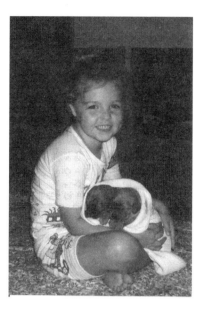

receipt for payment with promise to deliver the registration document within a short period of time. The breeder's document should contain the registered names and AKC numbers of both parents, date of birth of the litter, and puppy's color and sex. It should also indicate the type of registration you will be given: full (no breeding restrictions) or limited (no offspring of your puppy will be eligible for registration).

Both pedigree and registration papers are provided by a reputable breeder at no cost to the buyer. AKC does not allow the practice of charging an extra fee for registration papers, and any instance should be reported to them. Do not confuse this with a breeder's right to withhold papers until the dog has been spayed or neutered, which is how puppies not purchased for showing/breeding are often sold by reputable breeders. If the breeder is going to withhold the papers for this reason, that fact should be agreed upon in writing by both parties and stated in the contract.

▼ The breeder should give you written instructions on feeding, training, and care.

▼ The breeder should provide you proof that both the sire and dam of the litter have had their hips and elbows x-rayed and evaluated by OFA (Orthopedic Foundation of America) and received an OFA rating of Fair, Good, or Excellent or PennHIP evaluation.

▼ The breeder should provide you proof that the sire and dam have had their eyes examined by a board certified veterinary ophthalmologist within twelve to eighteen months of the breeding. He or she should also hand you proof that both parents were examined by a board certified veterinary cardiologist and are free of any heart defect.

▼ The breeder should be willing to answer your questions about any other possible hereditary problems including but not limited to seizures, hypothyroidism, skin problems, or allergies.

▼ The breeder should be able to give you references—names of people who have purchased puppies in the past, names of other breeders, and the veterinarian who provides care for the breeder's dogs.

▼ The breeder should provide some type of written contract with the conditions of sale and warranties. The warranty if any, should be absolutely explicit, and both parties should sign and receive a copy of the contract.

▼ The breeder should also make it clear that his or her responsibility continues long after you have taken your puppy home, in fact, as long as the dog is alive. If for any reason you are unable to keep the dog, many dedicated breeders will ask that the dog be returned to them so that they can find a new home, or they request that you obtain their approval of a new owner prior to placing the dog. Your breeder should be available for advice and encouragement whenever needed. This willingness on their part to be available for the life of your dog will help ease your way over many "rough spots."

What the Breeder Expects From You

▼ The breeder expects you to discuss your experience with dogs. For instance, the kind of dogs you have had in the past, whether you currently own a dog, what breed, age, etc., the age(s) of past dogs at time of death, and how the dogs died. They expect you to answer questions regarding your home, fencing, neighborhood, work, and lifestyle. They want an honest answer as to whether or not the dog will be allowed in the house and whether it will be considered a member of the family.

▼ The majority of reputable breeders are thorough and scrupulous in choosing homes for their "babies." The best interest of their puppies is always a priority. A returned puppy is a traumatic experience for all concerned, so the breeder who is willing to accept a puppy back will try to make absolutely certain that a golden retriever is the right breed for you and that you are willing to do everything possible to nurture and raise your puppy to be a loving, obedient companion and canine good citizen.

▼ Breeders all have their own criteria when placing puppies. Be sure to find out their criteria during your first conversation. This will save you both time and energy in the event that your home or lifestyle does not match that particular breeder's requirements.

How Much Does a Golden Retriever Cost?

A poorly bred, badly raised puppy, no matter how cheap, is no bargain! Chances are that the parents were not screened appropriately for hereditary defects, (hip, eye, heart) nor have the puppies had the appropriate veterinary care, socialization, and TLC that is needed to raise a healthy litter of golden puppies. Quite often this type of puppy costs as much or more than one purchased from a responsible hobby breeder. I recently learned of a person (not a reputable breeder) in Washington State who sold a litter of pet puppies for $1,000 each. The dam had no health clearances and no titles. I don't know who owned the stud dog, but it wasn't a reputable breeder, because he or she would not have bred a bitch without clearances and/or lack of quality! The old adage, "buyer beware," is so true when it comes to purchasing a golden puppy.

A properly raised pet puppy from good parentage sold on a spay/neuter contract or with AKC Limited Registration will generally sell from $700 to $1,000. The price may vary from region to region within the United States and Canada. It may also vary based upon the pedigree, status of the sire and/or dam, and the titles held by the parents and others in the pedigree. Puppies sold on show/breeding contracts may be priced the same as "pet" puppies, with additional provisions that take effect at a later date, i.e., more money paid when clearances are obtained, puppies given back after breeding. Show/breeding quality puppies are generally priced from $1,200 on up. Again, the price depends on the accomplishments of the parents and the pedigree. Generally, when a show/breeding quality puppy is sold, the price is greater, but then the warranties and promises made by the seller are also greater.

Male or Female—Does It Matter?

Temperamentally, there is little difference between the sexes in golden retrievers. Neither sex is harder to house train; both are equally intelligent and affectionate. Both are excellent with children, and both make excellent companions. Problems of aggressiveness, which males of other breeds may exhibit, rarely occur in the golden retriever. Sex-related behavior such as mounting and marking may be exhibited by some male goldens, particularly if other males are present or if the male has been used for breeding. Neutering a male before a year of age will not only help to alleviate these problems, but will also eliminate the potential for testicular cancer and lower the risk of prostate problems. Since there is no responsible reason not to spay a bitch (unless she was bought from a reputable breeder as potential breeding stock), the estrous cycle (heat, or in-season) need not be a consideration.

Picking Your Puppy

Once you have found a breeder that you trust, be prepared to place a deposit on a puppy. Good litters seldom go begging (that's why you don't see ads for these litters in the newspaper), and it is not uncommon for a choice litter to be completely spoken for by the time the puppies are seven weeks of age and ready to go to their new homes. Even if the breeder that you choose doesn't have puppies on the ground or a bitch that is due in the very near future, you may decide the wait is worth it. Plan to begin your search well in advance of the time you want to take the puppy home. This way, you can find the breeder and plan a vacation or at least a few days off when you bring your new baby home. Not all litters are created equally, not even well-bred litters. Some litters will be genetically predisposed for a higher energy level (remember our discussion on field/working dogs) and others for a lower energy level. Some litters will have a tendency to be more dominant and others more submissive. There will be differences among individual puppies in the same litter. Discuss with the breeder the type of dog you are looking for and how you expect it to fit into your lifestyle. Will the dog be a companion for small children, a hunting companion, or are you considering competing in obedience or conformation?

What to Look For

Almost all golden puppies are appealing, but you need to look for more than "cuteness." Look for the following.

▼ Build should be sturdy with straight legs.

▼ Body should feel firm and muscular.

▼ Puppy should be squirmy and active when first picked up, but be willing to relax and accept being held and cuddled for a short time.

▼ Coats should be clean and thick.

▼ Eyes, nose, and ears should be free of discharge or irritation.

▼ Puppy should NOT be potbellied (a sign it is full of worms.)

▼ Gums should be pink, not pale.

▼ Pigment around the eyes should be dark, with black nose and feet pads preferred, although this might not be important to you if the dog is being purchased strictly as a companion.

▼ No white or black markings are allowed for show/breeding stock, but, again, this does not affect the puppy's usefulness otherwise.

▼ Golden puppies are born much lighter than their adult color; even a very pale colored puppy will probably become a good gold shade. Look at the color of the ears—this is typically the color into which your puppy will mature.

▼ If the breeder offers you more than one puppy to select from, take each of the puppies you are considering (individually) away from the rest of its littermates and observe its reaction to its environment and to you. Puppies at seven to eight weeks of age should be willing to explore their environment. Although perhaps a little bit cautious at first, they should investigate new objects and be fairly self-assured. Speak to the puppy and see if it will follow you as you move away. Roll a ball or other toy, and see if it has the instinct to watch, chase, carry, and possibly even return to you with the ball. Some puppies are slower to develop the retrieving instinct than others, but you should not consider a puppy that does not show some interest or awareness of a moving object. See if the puppy exhibits the type of personality you would want to live with. Perhaps the bold, brash puppy that never stops getting into things would be too much for you, and the more easy-going fellow who's agreeable and a bit more receptive to your guidance would be a better choice.

Look at the Dam (Mother)

Don't forget to observe the dam as well. Any shyness or aggressiveness on her part may be indicative of a poor temperament, and the puppies might well inherit these undesirable traits. A golden retriever bitch should be watchful and patient with her puppies and should be happy to show them to you.

Breeder's Choice

I always let my potential owners know that I will be selecting their puppy for them. Why? Because I have lived with these babies for seven weeks; I've slept with them, played with them, groomed them, and spent hours observing them. I know each little puppy's personality. It's my responsibility to try and match each puppy's personality with the prospective owner. That is why it is important to get to know the new owners and observe them with the puppies before the final selection is made. As a potential owner, be prepared to listen to the advice of your breeder and let them select the puppy for you. If you find yourself in the position of having several to choose from, follow the instructions shown in "What To Look For," then follow your heart.

What to Avoid

When viewing potential puppies, you should avoid:

▼ Shy, whimpering, fearful puppies.

▼ Puppies with dull coats, crusty or running eyes, signs of diarrhea, rashes, or sores on their abdomens.

▼ Signs of neglect, such as lack of water, pans of uneaten food, dirty conditions.

▼ A breeder who will sell a puppy under the age of seven weeks (Day 49 forward is optimum), as early separation from the dam and littermates can be very detrimental both psychologically and physically.

Considering the Older Dog

If you aren't prepared to go through the trials and training of a baby puppy, acquiring an older puppy or even a mature dog can be a good alternative, especially in households in which the family pet may have to spend much of the day unsupervised. Golden retrievers are very adaptable, and a golden of any age with a good temperament, can become a member of the family in a very short time. There are many reasons that older dogs are available. Breeders often hold a puppy until it is old enough to determine its show or breeding potential; a female (brood bitch) that has been bred a couple of times is being retired and placed in a family home; or circumstances change and the breeder may be helping someone place a much-loved pet they have had to part with. The reasons are myriad, but whatever they may be, the grown dog is frequently available. He is most likely housebroken, knows many commands, and has formed many behavior patterns. If the dog has been loved and well taken care of, he will continue to offer love and devotion to his new owners because a properly raised golden loves and needs people. Never hesitate to take an outgoing, good-natured older dog into your home. Although it may be confused at first and carry a few problems, there is nothing that patience, consistency, and reassurance on

Jessie and Tank share a quiet moment

Photo: Cannon Goodnight

your part can't solve. The dog's self-confidence will return, and it will readily adapt to your routine.

Try to find out all you can about the older dog so that you can determine if his temperament is compatible with yours. Learn as much as possible about his habits, daily routine, likes and dislikes, diet, and medical history. It is important that all family members meet the dog to determine if this is the dog everyone wants to adopt. It is best to acquire the dog when the household member with the primary responsibility for the dog's care and training will be at home full time for the first few days. That way you can make it clear to the dog where it is to sleep, relieve itself, where and when it will eat, and what it can and cannot do in the house. In short, it has to learn the routine it will be following and what is expected of it.

Settling In

Give the dog a month or so to settle into its new environment and gain confidence in you before beginning formal obedience training. Even if the dog has had some obedience training, attending class is an excellent way to brush up on its training and help you understand its responses and personality more completely. Training together will strengthen your human/animal bond. It is also a good way for you to assess the dog's ability and help you decide if you want to pursue additional training in obedience, field, agility, tracking, etc.

If you rescue a mistreated or abandoned golden retriever through a Golden Retriever Club's Referral/Rescue Service (see Appendix for list) or a humane society and give it your affection, it will reward you with eternal love and gratitude. These dogs may be of unknown background and bring with them a few more problems than those with a more favorable history, but the rewards can be great. For additional information on acquiring a rescue golden retriever, call the GRCA National Information Line at 1-800-632-5155 or surf over to a list of rescue organizations on the GRCA web site: www.grca.org.

See Chapter 7, "Socialization and Training" for information about bringing home a rescue Golden Retriever

Chapter 5

Breeding the Golden Retriever

Before you dash off and buy a bitch puppy so you can have a litter of puppies, read on. If you've already purchased a puppy from a breeder who didn't care if your puppy was spayed or neutered, read on. If the breeder didn't ask you to sign your life away and promise to put titles on the dog, read on. If the breeder didn't require you to obtain all health clearances, test temperament, and evaluate structure before breeding, read on. If you believe in the Golden Rule: "Do unto others as you would have them do unto you," read on.

▼ So, You Want To Breed Your Dog?
▼ Consider Your Resources
▼ Consider Your Dog's Quality
▼ Considerations of the Stud Dog Owner
▼ Consider the Current Dog Population
▼ The Case for Spaying and Neutering
▼ Golden Retriever Club of America's Code of Ethics

So, You Want To Breed Your Dog?

Breeding is not for beginners. Doing it well is long hard work. It can be emotionally rewarding, but rarely is it profitable (unless you own a puppy mill). It is also risky. You can loose your precious bitch, generate huge veterinary bills, and miss a lot of sleep. You are doing the breed an injustice unless you consider all the following and are willing to abide by the Golden Retriever Club of America's Code of Ethics.

If you think that:

▼ *Having puppies would be fun,* realize it is also very time consuming and demanding. By four weeks of age, a golden litter of eight, twelve, or possibly even fourteen puppies is active, dirty, noisy, and potentially destructive. Illness or death of the dam or puppies can be expensive, emotional, and no fun at all.

▼ *It would be educational for the children,* consider that so would a litter of hamsters. Bitches do not whelp at your convenience, and the children are often in school or in bed at the time of delivery. Care of the pregnant bitch and properly raising and socializing puppies is work for a responsible adult.

Her whole world is in your hands

Photo: Cannon Goodnight

▼ *It would help us get back our investment,* you may find that the rate of return is very low. Stud fee, veterinary fees, advertising, and the daily care and feeding of a litter are very expensive. You may only be able to sell three or four puppies out of a litter of ten or twelve; even experienced breeders sometimes have difficulty selling puppies.

▼ *It would help fulfill the dog's needs,* you are anthropomorphizing. While the instinct for procreation is strong, the dog has no conscious knowledge of what it is missing, no regrets, and no guilt feelings. Spaying or neutering will remove the instinct and the problems often associated with it, such as wandering and marking. Pregnancy not only contributes nothing to a bitch's health, but sometimes it causes problems. A spayed bitch cannot be accidentally bred and will not be subject to the uterine infections common in older, intact females.

▼ *It will improve the bitch's temperament if she is bred,* you are wrong. No animal whose temperament needs improving should be bred in the first place, since temperament is most often the result of hereditary factors. Birthing and raising a litter will not only *not* make an improvement in the dam's temperament, it will also probably result in a litter of unsatisfactory puppies who have been imprinted by their unstable dam. There is also the possibility that the bitch will be an unsatisfactory mother, necessitating much more work on your part.

Consider Your Resources

Raising a litter is a demanding project. Before proceeding, consider carefully the following questions:

▼ *Do you have the facilities for whelping and raising a litter properly?* You need a warm, quiet, secure area, which is easily cleaned, for properly confining and caring for a litter of eight, ten, or twelve fast-growing puppies while they are with their mother and a similar, much larger, area for use after weaning.

▼ *Do you have the time to devote to this project?* Time to take or send a bitch for breeding, sit up for hours during whelping, and hand raise the litter if the bitch is unable to? Time to buy and prepare food, feed, and clean up four or five times daily? Time to go to the veterinarian for checkups, inoculations, or to evaluate a sick dam or puppy? Time to scrub floors and pens, clean up feces and urine, and give medication—two or three times a day? Time to individually socialize each puppy daily? Time to answer phone calls, talk with prospective buyers, and answer the same questions over and over again? Time for all the paperwork required, including typing accurate pedigrees, health records, care instructions, records of sales, and so on?

▼ *Do you have the money to put into the project?* Can you afford to pay the stud fee ($700-1,000), inoculations and veterinary care for the bitch and puppies, as well as other expenses? ($500 and more) What if the bitch has problems that necessitate a caesarean section? ($500-$750) What if the puppies die? (A tragedy!) What if the bitch dies (an even worse tragedy!) or cannot raise the puppies? (Be prepared to feed round the clock for three weeks.) Can you afford to feed and provide veterinary care for two- or three- or four-month-old puppies that didn't sell? Can you afford to refund the purchase price on a puppy that proves to be unsound or unsuitable?

Consider Your Dog or Bitch's Quality

Is your dog truly an outstanding representative of the breed? Pretty, friendly, and smart is not nearly enough.

Temperament

Your dog must be absolutely sound and stable, with a personality and disposition appropriate for the breed. Shyness, aggressiveness, gun shyness, lack of retrieving ability or trainability, and hyperactivity are all reasons not to breed, regardless of other qualities.

Breed Type and Quality

Your dog must be structurally and functionally sound, with conformation characteristics appropriate for the breed. An experienced, knowledgeable exhibitor/breeder can assist in the evaluation of your dog's adherence to the breed standard.

Soundness

Your dog should be tested free of certain genetic defects, as should the proposed mate. Knowledge of the status of parents, grandparents, siblings, etc. with regard to genetic testing is also desirable. Hips should be properly x-rayed, and the x-rays submitted to the Orthopedic Foundation for Animals or PennHIP to be read as free of hip dysplasia. Hearts should be examined by a board-certified cardiologist. Eyes should be examined annually by a board- certified veterinary ophthalmologist and be free of hereditary cataracts, progressive retinal atrophy, and any other eye anomaly.

Pedigree

A four or five generation pedigree on the proposed litter should be read and interpreted by a person with extensive knowledge of the breed and of the dogs involved. Titles alone are no guarantee of genetic value. Any inheritable defects, including but not limited to retained testicles, overshot or undershot jaw, congenital heart defects, recurrent skin problems, thyroid deficiency, immunological problems and recurrent seizures or epilepsy occurring in either parent are all reasons not to breed, regardless of other qualities.

Health

A breeding animal must be fully mature, in the prime of health, and in lean muscular condition. All inoculations should be up to date, and the animal should be free of both internal and external parasites. Acquired problems such as narrow birth canal from previous injury, canine brucellosis, transmissible venereal tumor, anemia, any disease or infection of the reproductive organs, concurrent diseases of other organ systems, or any contagious diseases are all reasons not to breed.

Considerations of the Stud Dog Owner

If you are thinking of using your male at stud, you are no less responsible for the quality of the litter than the owner of the brood bitch. You have the obligation of thoroughly screening every owner that inquires for stud service and the bitch to be bred; of traveling to and from the airport to pick up and return bitches sent in for breeding; of boarding and caring for bitches that are sent to you; of carrying out the breeding; of supplying pedigrees, photos, and examination reports; and of keeping meticulous records. This is all done as circumstances dictate, and not at your convenience; the weekend away you had planned may well be spent at home looking after a visiting bitch instead.

Consider the Dog Population

If, at this point, you are still considering breeding your dog, visit the dog pound, humane society, or animal shelter in the city nearest you. Ask how many dogs are euthanized monthly and how many euthanized in the last month were golden retrievers.

The Case for Spaying or Neutering

Many reputable breeders sell "pet" quality puppies with the agreement that the animal will be neutered. These puppies are sometimes sold at a lower price than the "show prospect" puppies, even though they have the same excellent pedigree and have received the same care and attention. The basic disposition and temperament of your dog WILL NOT be changed by removing his or her reproductive capability. Neutering a male can make him more tolerant of other males, but neutering will not, by itself, turn your golden into an obese, lazy animal—that is the result of excess food and insufficient exercise.

Benefits of spaying include not having to worry about accidental breedings, the stress and inconvenience of confining the bitch in season, risky "mismating" shots, and unwanted puppies. The spayed bitch will not develop uterine infections or tumors of the reproductive system, as do so many older unspayed bitches.

The American Kennel Club permits spayed and neutered goldens to participate in all phases of obedience, tracking, field work, agility, and junior handling, but not in most conformation classes.

GRCA Code of Ethics

The Golden Retriever Club of America endorses the following Code of Ethics for its members. It is the purpose of GRCA to encourage its members to perfect through selection, breeding, and training the type of dog most suitable in all respects for work as a companionable gun dog, and to do all in its power to protect and advance the interests of golden retrievers in every endeavor.

Responsibilities as a Dog Owner

Members must ensure that their dogs are kept safe and under control at all times. Members should properly train their dogs so that they are an asset to their community and not a nuisance. Dogs must be maintained with their safety and good health in mind at all times, including adequate and appropriate attention and socialization, grooming, feeding, veterinary attention, housing, routine care, exercise, and training.

Responsibilities as a Member of GRCA

Members' responsibilities include educating the public about the breed, keeping in mind that they and their dogs represent the breed, GRCA, and the sport of purebred dogs in general. Members are urged to accept the written breed standard as approved by the American Kennel Club (or the other applicable governing body of the country in which they reside or exhibit) as the standard description of physical and temperamental qualities by which the golden retriever is to be judged. Members are required to maintain good sportsmanship at all events and competitions, abiding by the applicable rules and regulations set forth by the governing bodies for such events and competitions. Members' conduct should always be in accord with the purposes and intent of the GRCA Constitution and Bylaws.

Responsibilities as a Breeder

GRCA members who breed golden retrievers are encouraged to maintain the purpose of the breed and are expected to demonstrate honesty and fairness in dealing with other owners and breeders, purchasers of dogs, and the general public. Owners of breeding animals shall provide appropriate documentation to all concerned regarding the health of dogs involved in a breeding or sale, including reports of examinations such as those applying to hips and eyes. If any such examinations have not been performed on a dog, this should be stated. Breeders should understand and acknowledge that they may need to take back, or assist in finding a new home for, any dog they produce at any time in its life, if requested to do so.

Members who breed should sell puppies, permit stud service, and/or lease any stud dogs or brood bitches only to individuals who give satisfactory evidence that they will give proper care and attention to the animals concerned and who may be expected generally to act within the intent of the statements of this Code of Ethics. Members are encouraged to use clear, concise written contracts to document the sale of animals, use of stud dogs, and lease arrangements, including the use, when appropriate, of non-breeding agreements, and/or limited registration. Members should not sell dogs at auction or to brokers or commercial dealers.

Advisory Guidelines

Breeding stock should be selected with the objects of GRCA in mind, that is:

> Recognizing that the golden retriever breed was developed as a useful gun dog, to encourage the perfection by careful and selective breeding of golden retrievers that possess the appearance, structure, soundness, temperament, natural ability, and personality that are characterized in the standard of the breed, and to do all possible to advance and promote the perfection of these qualities. (Paraphrased from Article I, Section 2, of the GRCA Bylaws, as amended in 1995.) GRCA members are expected to follow AKC

requirements for record keeping, identification of animals, and registration procedures. Animals selected for breeding should:

(i) be of temperament typical of the golden retriever breed; stable, friendly, trainable, and willing to work. Temperament is of utmost importance to the breed and must never be neglected;

(ii) be in good health, including freedom from communicable disease;

(iii) possess the following examination reports in order to verify status concerning possible hip dysplasia, hereditary eye disease, or cardiovascular disease.

Hips: appropriate report from Orthopedic Foundation for Animals; PennHip; Ontario Veterinary College; BVA/KC Hip Score (Great Britain) or at least a written report from a board-certified veterinary radiologist (Diplomate of the American College of Veterinary Radiologists).

Eyes: appropriate report from a Diplomate of the American College of Veterinary Ophthalmology (ACVO) or from a BVA/KC approved ophthalmologist (Great Britain).

Hearts: appropriate report from a Diplomate of the American College of Veterinary Medicine, Cardiology Specialty. Consideration should be given also to other disorders that may have a genetic component, including, but not limited to, epilepsy, hypothyroidism, skin disorders (allergies), and orthopedic disorders such as elbow dysplasia and osteochondritis.

(iv) Assuming all health and examination reports are favorable, the age of the breeding pair also is of consideration. Generally, a golden retriever is not physically and mentally mature until the age of two years; an individual dog's suitability as a breeding animal is difficult to assess until that time.

Author's Note

Elbow Clearances: The GRCA has adopted a resolution that any dog or bitch advertised as breeding stock must provide evidence of hip, elbow, eye, and heart clearances on file before an advertisement will be accepted.

Membership Application: A copy of the most current GRCA membership application can be found in the Appendix. You may use this to apply for membership in the GRCA. Membership includes a subscription to the *GRNews* magazine.

Chapter 6
Adjusting to Life
With a Golden Retriever

In the following sections, we'll deal with all the issues that involve your dog's adjustment to his new life and your role in training him to be an obedient, confident, and loving member of the family.

▼ Stages of Growth
▼ Housetraining
▼ Crate Training
▼ Fencing
▼ Traveling

Scandal's favorite hiding place

Photo: Brandye Randermann

Stages of Growth

Seven Weeks of Age

This is a particularly significant time for a puppy. A seven-week-old golden retriever is trainable, emotionally ready to learn, and still dependent, however, his neurological system is not completely developed. Final development occurs toward the end of the seventh week. During this critical period what he learns will influence his attitude toward other animals and people. This is the time when a dog develops his ability to form a strong human bond. This is the reason that most breeders attempt to place their puppies in their new homes at day forty-nine. It gives them time to settle, bond, and have positive influences during this critical stage of development.

My policy is if a puppy is going to live with a family living in my immediate area, I send the puppy to their new home at this time (day forty-nine or fifty). If for some reason I can't get the puppy to its new home during this period, such as a long distance trip by auto or airline is required, I wait until he is nine weeks old. During that eighth week, I keep the puppy's stress level at a minimum and give him lots of love and individual attention.

Eight to Twelve Weeks

Puppies need human contact and companionship from owners, children, and other SAFE dogs during this critical stage. This is the time to begin simple commands and gentle discipline. This is the time when your puppy learns to TRUST YOU! The simple commands I teach at this time are "OFF" (always useful with a golden), "WAIT," "OK," and "SIT."

For instructions on basic training, see the "Obedience" section of Chapter 11.

Thirteen to Sixteen Weeks

During this time, show your puppy that you love him or her implicitly, however, *make sure he understands you are the top dog— number one*—numero uno! Each puppy will take a different measure of discipline. What is suitable for one puppy may be too forceful for another. By this time, you should know your puppy's

Hula and KC—13 weeks old.   *Photo: Jerry Vavra*

personality. Is he or she gentle, a bit soft, and quick to respond to correction or praise? Perhaps he or she is full of mischief, confident, rambunctious, a tease, running the other way so you have to catch him or her. One puppy will take very little correction before "folding"—which you don't want. The other is "tougher" and will take it and may even be stubborn about "taking" it. If you need help figuring out how much is enough and how much is too much, talk to your breeder or seek the advice of your veterinarian or a training instructor in your local area. Now is the time to enroll in basic obedience classes.

Nine to Eighteen Months

Ah, puberty. You remember those awesome teen-age years, don't you? If not, your puppy will help remind you. Golden retrievers are slow to mature. Male goldens are physically mature by four years of age, and bitches are typically mature by the age of three. Mentally, they are generally mature by the age of two. Puppies that are spayed or neutered tend to have an easier time during this period, as the hormones are not as active. Expect your puppy to still "act like a puppy." It is still too early for long walks on a leash or jogging. Even though he looks BIG, his bones and joints are still not mature. Mentally, he's still a puppy. Some days you'll marvel at his or her intelligence, and other days you'll be scratching your head wondering why you ever decided to get a dog!

One thing I have noticed with a couple of my "teens" is that some time around the age of nine months, they became fearful of situations in which they previously had been comfortable and confident. Typically, they seemed to regress in age, and they acted as if the (very familiar) situation was a whole new experience. If you experience this with your dog, it is very important that you recognize the symptoms and begin to recondition him or her. This will take patience and persistence. You will need to be sensitive to the dog's stress, but don't baby him or her. Reintroduce your "teen" to the situation over and over again until his or her fear is reduced to nothing.

House Training

Dogs are den animals, so they do not want to go to the bathroom where they live. Unfortunately, most of us live in homes that are so big the dog does not equate the entire house with his den. Therefore, it is important to keep the dog in the room that you are in. If you let him leave the room, he will equate this with leaving the den and think it is acceptable to go to the bathroom. If you are in the bedroom, shut him in the bedroom with you. If you go to the kitchen, take him with you. If it is not possible to shut a door, put up a baby gate or tie him in the room.

"Comet" learning to accept confinement

Photo courtesy of the author

Activities Not Clocks

Don't watch the clock to determine when your dog needs to go outside; it is her activity that causes her to need to go to the bathroom, not the time that has elapsed. Every time your dog changes activities, she should be taken outside. If she wakes up, take her outside. When she stops playing, out she goes. As soon as she stops eating, out again. Take her out BEFORE an accident occurs.

Watch for Signals

Do not think it is the dog's responsibility to let you know when she needs to go out; try to watch for her signals to you that she needs to go outside. The signals may be subtle, like walking in circles or walking toward the door sniffing.

Accidents

If the dog does go to the bathroom in the house while you are not watching, there is absolutely nothing you can do to correct the dog. Why? Dogs do not remember or feel responsible for actions in the past. If you drag a dog to an old mess and make a fuss, he does not say to himself, "I went to the bathroom here twenty minutes ago, which is why my owner is upset." Instead, he records the situation in his mind and makes sure the situation does not occur again. How? In this case, the dog records, "If my owner is present, and I am present, and a mess is present, I'll get scolded." Result—the next time there is a mess on the floor and he hears you coming, he will run.

Situations

Our tendency is to give the dog human reasoning abilities and emotions. Often owners will say, "I know my dog realized he was bad; he ran from me, and he looked guilty." He is NOT running from you because he understands that he is responsible for the mess, but because he realizes that if he stays in the situation that includes him, you, and the mess, he will be scolded.

Facts Relating to House Training

A seven- to eight-week golden retriever will need to eliminate immediately after eating, drinking water, and waking up. Your puppy does not want to eliminate in his or her eating or sleeping area. Each week as he grows, he will be able to "hold" it for longer periods of time. By the time he is ten weeks old, he will be able to "hold" it for six to seven hours at night, if confined to his crate. During the day, when he is in the house with you, use the schedule shown below to facilitate his training and ease the wear and tear on your home.

Helpful Hints

Purchase a large bottle of liquid enzyme. It is available at any pet supply store or through a supply catalog. Brands such as *Outright* and *Nature's Miracle* will remove stain and odors from carpets.

Rules of the Game

▼ *DON'T* allow your puppy free access to the house without constant supervision.

▼ *DON'T* expect full control of elimination before the age of four months.

▼ *DON'T* expect your puppy to be completely house trained before the age of six months.

▼ *DON'T* let your puppy see you clean up his mess.

▼ *DON'T* rub your puppy's nose in his poop. This is degrading and teaches nothing.

▼ *DON'T* overfeed your puppy. This results in loose stools and lack of control.

▼ *DO* be consistent, prompt, and always praise for a job well done.

▼ *DO* expect your puppy to make mistakes. However, remember, he is eager to please you, and with the proper training and frequent exercise, he will learn quickly. If you question the validity of this statement, pour a glass of water on the floor and talk to the dog in the same tone of voice you use when you find a mess on the floor. He will undoubtedly slink away from you just as he does when the mess is his. This should prove to you that it is not his guilt that makes him leave, but your reaction to the situation.

▼ *DO* enclose your puppy in a run, a crate, or a small room where she will not be punished if she eliminates. Short periods of time in a crate or similar area will encourage her to "hold it" rather than mess in her living quarters.

▼ *DO* keep a regular schedule of feeding and going outside to eliminate seven days a week. If on the weekends his routine is different, he will become confused. You CANNOT expect to confine a young puppy for eight hours during the day and not have him eliminate. You CAN expect a puppy of nine weeks or more, who is crate trained, to sleep through the night. Here is a sample schedule:

Feed—5:00 to 6:00 p.m.
Exercise—10:00 to 11:00 p.m.
Water—Restrict intake after 8:00 p.m.

▼ *DO* anticipate your puppy's needs and catch him before he makes a mistake.

▼ *DO* try to catch your pup in the middle of eliminating in the wrong spot. Quickly remove him to the right area. Quickly is the key word here, because in a few seconds, your puppy forgets his mistake. Do not correct; remember he does not have the ability to reason like a human.

Stain Removal Recipe

1 cup of hydrogen peroxide
1 teaspoon of ammonia

Mix and use within one-half hour of mixing. It is no good after that. Dab the mixture on the stain. Place white paper towel (do not use paper towel with color design) over the stain, and weigh it down with something. Leave for 2 to 3 hours; the stain will be gone.

Reprinted with permission of Dave Larsen

A Guide To Crate Training

A crate is an essential piece of equipment both for you and your golden retriever. Don't argue, don't feel that you are punishing your dog, just keep reading and trust me!

What Is a Dog Crate?

A dog crate is an enclosure with a top and a door. Crates are made in a variety of sizes proportioned to fit any type of dog. They are constructed of wire, wood, metal, or molded plastic/ fiberglass. Their purpose is to provide guaranteed safety and security for travel, confinement in case of illness or injury, assistance in house training, and a place of solitude for your pet.

Dog crates are trusted and used extensively by dog show exhibitors, obedience and field trial competitors, trainers, breeders, groomers, veterinarians, and anyone else who handles dogs regularly.

Many dog owners believe that the crate is "like a jail," that it's cruel. If this is your first reaction to using a crate, you are a very typical pet owner. As a reasoning human being, you really value your freedom; since you consider your pet an extension of your family, it is only natural to feel that closing him or her in a crate is inhumane. Perhaps you believe that your dog will grow to hate you or that you are creating psychological damage. You DO NOT think like a dog.

If your dog could talk to you he or she would say, "I love having a room of my own. It's my private special place, my security blanket." He or she would also tell you that the crate helps satisfy his or her "den instinct." This den instinct was inherited from his den-dwelling ancestors and relatives. He would further admit that he is much happier and more secure having his life controlled and structured by you. He would rather be prevented from causing trouble than be punished for it. To you it may be a cage, but to your dog, it's a home.

Wire crate

Airline approved crate

The Advantages of Using a Crate

A dog crate, correctly and humanely used, can have many advantages for both you and your pet.

▼ You can enjoy complete peace of mind when leaving your dog alone, knowing that nothing will be soiled or destroyed.

▼ You can housebreak your dog more quickly by using the crate to encourage control and establish a regular routine for outdoor elimination.

▼ You can effectively confine your dog at times when his presence may be disruptive such as during family activities, meal times, when guests or workers are present, and when he is overexcited or bothered by too much activity or by children.

▼ You can travel with your dog without risk of distraction for the driver or injury to persons in the vehicle. It also prevents him from getting out of the vehicle to become lost or injured.

▼ Your dog can enjoy the privacy and security of his own den to which he can retreat when tired, stressed, or ill.

▼ Your dog can be spared the loneliness and frustration of having to be isolated in the basement, garage, or other outside area.

▼ Your dog can be conveniently included in family outings, visits, and trips instead of being left behind alone at home or in a boarding kennel.

Where Should I Put the Crate?

Since the main reason for using a crate is to confine a dog without making him or her feel isolated or banished, it should be placed near a "people area." The kitchen or family room of a home is generally the most convenient. Place the crate in a corner or next to a sofa. You can even put a pretty cloth on top and use it as a table, which I do. Admittedly, a dog crate is not a "thing of beauty," but it can be forgiven as it proves how much it can help the dog remain a welcome addition to the household.

Where Can I Get a Crate?

New crates can be purchased in pet supply stores, feed stores, at dog shows, and from catalogs. Ordering from a catalog will usually save you money.

What Type of Crate Is Best?

The most practical dog crate for use by the pet owner is a collapsible wire mesh type available in a variety of sizes. They are lightweight and easily handled, and they allow for total ventilation. The dog can see everything going on around her. If you want to restrict her view or give her more privacy, you may purchase a fitted cover that allows for ventilation or place a sheet or cloth over the crate for short periods of time. Most wire crates include a removable metal pan or tray. You will probably want to purchase a crate pad for added comfort. They come in sizes to fit the various brands of crates. I have found dogs like the pads with synthetic sheepskin on the top in the winter, and during the summer, they like pads constructed from "patio furniture" like the cushions found on patio furniture. They seem to be cool in the summer and warm in the winter.

Another type of crate is the one with which you are probably most familiar. It is an "airline approved" crate made of fiberglass. These are very safe and make excellent dens for any dog. If you plan to travel with your dog by air, you will need this type of crate. When traveling in an SUV or station wagon with large portions of glass, your dog may be safer in this type of crate; in the event the glass should break, the dog is better protected.

Customize Your Crate

I make a crate bottom that fits inside my airline-type crates. This fits in and rests over the hump that is always found on the bottom of these crates. Make the bottom from pegboard found at your local builder's supply. Have it cut to the inside dimension of the crate. You can put ice under it in the summer, and the dog will remain cool, and it provides a comfortable place to rest without the heat created by a pad. GOLDENS LIKE TO BE COOL.

What Size Should a Crate Be?

A crate should always be large enough to allow any dog to stretch out flat on his or her side, to sit or stand without hitting his or her head on the top, to turn around, and to otherwise feel that he or she has freedom of movement. Equip the crate with a clip-on water dish. If using the airline-type crate, a golden retriever adult male is most comfortable in a #500 size, and females need the #400.

I personally recommend using a smaller crate for puppies and graduating to a larger size at maturity. If you don't want to purchase more than one crate, use the formula above to decide what size crate to purchase. Check with friends and neighbors to see if they have a smaller size.

Crate Training Your Puppy

Establish a crate routine by closing the puppy in at regular one to two hour intervals during the day. His own chosen nap times will guide you. Crate him whenever he must be left alone (no more than four hours). Do not leave his collar on!

When first crate training your puppy at night, you may prefer to place the crate, with the door left open and newspapers nearby, in a small enclosed area such as a bathroom or laundry room. If you prefer, you may place the crate in your bedroom with the door closed, but expect that the pup will wake around three to four a.m. to eliminate. Take him outside, and then put him back in the crate until seven a.m. Somewhere between nine and ten weeks of age, your puppy will be sleeping through the night. Even if things do not go smoothly at first, don't weaken and don't worry. Be consistent, be firm, and be very aware that you are doing your pet a real favor by preventing him from getting into trouble while left alone.

If you don't want to use a crate permanently, plan to use it for at least five to six months until the puppy is well past the teething stage. At that point, you may start leaving the crate door open at night, when someone is at home during the day, or when he is briefly alone. If all goes well for a week or two, and the dog seems reliable when left alone, remove the crate itself and leave the bedding in the same spot.

The dog will probably miss the crate enclosure, but that spot will have become "his own place," and his habit of good behavior should continue. However, should "problem behavior" begin anew, you'll want to rethink your decision to forego use of the crate. Even after a long period without a crate, a dog that has been raised in one will readily accept it should the need arise.

Use But Don't Abuse

The use of a dog crate is not recommended for a dog that must be frequently or regularly left alone for an extended time, for instance, all or much of the day while the owner is away at work or school. If this is attempted, the dog must be exercised before and after crating, given lots of personal positive attention, and allowed complete freedom at night, including sleeping near his owner.

Fool-Proof Method for Getting Your Dog into the Crate

Throw a small biscuit into the crate and say, "kennel up." Your dog will "fly" into his crate. When the dog is crate trained and goes in on command, continue to give the biscuit as a reward after he is in the crate.

Crating the Adult Dog

Much of the problem behavior of an older puppy (over six months) or an adult dog is caused by the lack of a feeling of security when left alone. Although a crate can fulfill this need and hopefully solve the problem, it still must be introduced gradually.

Every possible effort must be made to ensure that the dog's first association with the crate is very positive and pleasant. Again, I want to stress that the dog crate is not intended for frequent long hours of use by an absent owner.

Place a crate of adequate size in a location where the dog will feel part of the human family. Secure the crate door open so that it can't unexpectedly shut and frighten him or her. Encourage the dog to investigate this new object thoroughly, luring him or her inside by tossing tidbits of cheese, liver, or hot dog into the crate. Give him or her free access to come and go as he or she pleases. Leave special toys in the crate. If the dog drags them out to play with them, that is ok. Just keep putting them back in from time to time, treating the crate like the dog's "toy box."

When he begins to enter the crate confidently, place his bedding in the crate, and coax him to lie down and relax, still using food, if necessary. Continue this pattern for several days, encouraging him to use the crate as much as possible and shutting the door briefly while you sit beside him or there are people visiting and he can hear your voices. Do not hesitate to meet modest resistance with consistent firmness.

When you are confident that the dog will remain quietly in the closed crate, you may safely leave him alone. Make sure he has chew toys that are safe and that he is not wearing a collar. If you are uncertain or anxious, leave him at first for brief periods, one-half to one hour, until he has proved that he will not resist confinement.

> **A WORD OF CAUTION:** The use of a dog crate is intended to help in forming a well-balanced, emotionally healthy dog. Crate or no crate, any dog constantly denied the human companionship it needs and craves is going to be a lonely pet and will find ways to express anxiety, depression, and stress.

Please Fence Me In!

Most reputable breeders will not place a golden retriever in a home that does not have some type of secure enclosure to protect the dog. This is certainly my policy. I want the fence installed before the puppy goes to its new home. I recognize that many people who own dogs do not have an enclosure, however, consider these three facts.

Fact 1   Your dog will be safe and secure from harm and theft.

Fact 2   You will not suffer the consequences of a legal action should your dog injure or hurt another dog or person.

Fact 3   You will have peace of mind when you are away from home. There are many ways to safely contain a dog so that both the dog and the owner are satisfied.

Chainlink kennel run   *Courtesy PetEdge*

The following are suggestions that have worked for me and other responsible dog owners.

A Kennel Run

A chain link dog kennel run is one of the safest environments for your dog. You can purchase the components for a fully portable kennel run from a home improvement store for as little as $300. These easy-to-set-up panels are six feet high, ten to twelve feet long on the sides, and six by six feet at each end. They come complete with hardware and can be put together in thirty minutes.

No Digging Out!

Placing the run on concrete is one of the easiest and safest methods for "dig proofing" your kennel run. If the run is on concrete, it is a good idea to create a space for the dog to lie down so that he or she can get off the concrete. Some of the alternatives are a bale of shavings, a horse trailer/stall mat (these are tough rubber and virtually indestructible), a raised platform, or a raised bed (available from dog supply catalogs).

If the dog is going to be out for long periods of time, place a doghouse or large airline kennel in the run so he or she has a den in which to retreat. Cover at least one-half of the kennel run with a roof, tarp, or shade screen so that the dog has relief from the elements.

Other Alternatives

If you have to install your kennel on a dirt surface, you will need to make sure the dog can't dig out along the edge of the run. Here are two solutions.

1.   Purchase a piece of cyclone fencing cut a little larger than the dimensions of the kennel. (You can usually find used fencing from a fence contractor for a fraction of the price of new.) Lay the chain link on the ground, and place the kennel run on top. Cover the chain link with pea gravel or bark, and you have a secure environment.

2.   Dig a narrow ditch about twelve inches deep just inside the fence line around the entire perimeter of the run. Insert cement building blocks placed end to end along the perimeter and fill with dirt. Place your pea gravel or playground bark over the dirt.

Even if you have a fully fenced back yard, I recommend that you install a kennel run. The run provides protection for your dog if there are children playing in the yard and the gate is left open. It provides a secure place to leave the dog when you are not home. It will prevent the dog from digging or eating plants that may be harmful or fatal.

The run can be as simple as a gravel strip next to the garage against an existing fence with a secure gate and some cover. The possibilities are endless. A thorough review of your home and property will usually offer you several alternatives.

Invisible Fencing–Low Voltage

If you live in a neighborhood where a traditional fenced yard is not practical or allowed due to covenants or restrictions, I suggest installing a kennel run in an unobtrusive area where it cannot be seen from the street and purchasing and installing one of the new underground fencing systems.

These systems consist of wire installed several inches below the ground around the perimeter of the area you wish to contain. They have an electric sensor, and the dog wears a collar with another sensor attached. Available from various sources, they cost anywhere from $200-$500. Installation is relatively simple.

You may also purchase one from a fencing contractor specializing in electronic fences.

With this type of fence, your dog learns the boundaries of his or her area and wears a collar that emits a warning beep. If the dog continues to enter the boundary, it will receive a mild shock through the collar. Though I have not used this system, I have had glowing reports from others who find them a useful and effective means of containing their dogs.

The "Obedience" section of Chapter 11 contains instructions for training your golden retriever to the underground fence system.

> **Warning: When using this type of system, DO NOT leave the dog outside alone. This type of fence will contain your dog; it will not keep other dogs out. "Home alone" with this type of fence puts your dog at the mercy of other dogs or people who may wish to harm or steal him.**

Unless you are home with your dog ALL THE TIME, he or she will need a safe place to stay when you are gone. It won't be practical to leave him or her in the house alone for long periods when he or she is a puppy, and it might not be practical when he or she is an adult. So, what do you do? If you can't put a kennel run anywhere outside your home, put it in your garage. Even if you purchase a smaller size (for shorter periods of time), do yourself a favor and get a kennel run. No garage? Put it on your back deck or patio. Many of my clients live on golf courses, along the water, in the country, or in other areas that have CC&Rs that restrict fences. The combination of the electronic fence system and the kennel run provides a safe and humane way of protecting your dog.

Don't Let This Happen to Your Dog!

Here is a true story of what happened to a beautiful boxer by the name of Bowser whose owners relied on electronic fencing to safely contain him.

Bowser lived in a very nice residential area on an estate-sized lot with electronic fencing, and he had the run of the property while his owners were at work. Residing several streets away was a family with two chow chow dogs, and one day the dogs got loose. They ran the neighborhood, discovered Bowser, entered the yard, and attacked him. He was horribly mauled, and though the veterinarian tried to save him, he died twenty-four hours after the attack.

Traveling With Your Dog

"Ready to Go"   *Photo: Valerie Anderson*

Traveling with your dog is great fun for all concerned; golden retrievers love to travel! In order to do it right, you need certain equipment, and you must use it all the time.

Traveling Safely

The average golden retriever weighs approximately the same as a ten-year-old child. As a responsible adult, you do not allow a ten-year-old child to ride without a seat belt. You do not allow your babies or small children to ride without benefit of a car seat or restraint. Neither should you allow your dog to ride without some type of restraint for protection. In case of an emergency stop or an accident, a large dog loose in the vehicle can cause injury or even death to the passengers in the vehicle. Even if passengers are not injured, an unrestrained dog will be.

If you like your golden to ride in the front or rear seat, purchase a specially made harness that attaches to the seat belt in your vehicle. These cost between twelve and fifteen dollars and are available at pet supply stores or through the wholesale catalogs.

> *CAUTION: Most autos and trucks now have airbags. If your dog is sitting in the front, an airbag may severely injure or kill him! Place the dog in the back seat with a proper restraint.*

If you own a minivan, station wagon, or other similar vehicle, I recommend that you purchase an airline-type crate and let the dog travel in his crate. Secure the crate with web nylon tie-downs so that in case of an emergency, the crate does not fly around the back of the van or fly forward over the seats.

You might also consider putting in a barrier for added security. If you don't want to put the dog in a crate, at least purchase a metal wire barrier. These barriers are adjustable and fit any type vehicle that has a deck in the rear. You can barricade the dog in the back portion of the vehicle yet still see and touch him.

Hot Weather

When the weather is warm, traveling with your dog takes planning and awareness on your part. A vehicle absorbs heat and retains it. If the temperature outside is eighty degrees it can, within a matter of ten minutes, reach 110 degrees inside the vehicle. This will cause a dog to die of heat stroke. Here are some suggestions for dealing with the heat.

▼ If you are going to be out of the vehicle for any length of time and it is not necessary for the dog to be with you, leave him home.

▼ Run your air conditioner so the car is cool when you leave. Park in the shade, and leave the windows partially down. Better yet, purchase some plastic grill inserts for several windows. These are available at pet supply stores or through a catalog. These inserts allow you to roll down the windows. They also keep the dog from jumping out of the car and give you an extra measure of safety.

▼ Lock your car. There are many people who would love to steal your golden. Recently, a friend of mine took his beautiful champion golden retriever with him to the corner store. The dog was left sitting on the front seat of the car for three minutes. When the owner returned, the dog was gone. Stolen! After several days of agony and a one thousand dollar reward, the dog was recovered.

▼ Provide a water dish containing fresh water, and if possible, add ice cubes to the water.

▼ Place a shade screen over your front window and the rear window if necessary. You can also use shade cloth purchased from a home improvement store. Cut it to fit the shape of the window, and attach it to visors or any other available surface with clothespins or small alligator clips.

Bottled Water

If you are traveling long distances and will be stopping to "air" your dog and give it water, do one of two things: 1) bring a gallon or two of water from home; or 2) if you will be gone more than a day or two, purchase bottled water for the entire trip. It is very common for dogs to experience intestinal upset when their water is changed. Believe me, there is nothing worse for you or for the dog then having diarrhea in the crate.

Car Sickness

Dogs generally become sick in the car because they are frightened, not because they have real motion sickness. It is necessary to reassure your dog that these fears are groundless (which might be hard depending on how you drive). You need to get your dog used to the car by taking trips that are short enough that your dog does not exhibit the typical signs of car sickness—drooling, vomiting, etc. It may be necessary to start out by just sitting in the car together and giving your dog a treat after a few minutes. Then take very short rides followed by a treat—even if you can only make it to the end of the driveway. Gradually increase the length of the trips until your dog enjoys the car rides.

Chapter 7

Socialization and Basic Training

Look at you! You know how to crate train and house train a dog. You understand the importance of containing your dog, and you're ready to travel together. Give yourself a pat on the back, and get ready to help your golden become a "canine good citizen."

▼ Socializing Your Dog
▼ Group Training Classes
▼ Toys and Other Endearing Objects
▼ Just for Parents
▼ Just For Kids
▼ Puppy's First Day
▼ Bringing Home Your Adopted Rescue Golden Retriever
▼ The Canine Good Citizen

Socializing Your Dog

If you purchased your golden retriever from a reputable breeder, you can be assured that it was handled constantly, brushed and groomed, exposed to noises and other dogs, and kissed at least a thousand times.

Joel and Maureen enjoy the backcountry

Photo: Pat Anderson

The Breeder's Responsibility

Most breeders wean their puppies between the ages of five and six weeks of age. Weaning is the process of taking the puppies away from their mother's milk. Generally all nursing stops by the time puppies are six and one-half weeks of age. At weaning, the breeder becomes the puppies' caretaker and role model. Many hours of each day are devoted to the care and well-being of the puppies. Everything possible has been done to prepare them for their new life so that they are ready to give and receive devotion, loyalty, and love.

It's Your Turn

When you take your puppy home, it becomes your responsibility to see that his or her education continues. It is important that you handle the specific periods of his or her young life with knowledge and care. These periods shape and mold his or her character and much of his or her personality.

Where to Begin

▼ Begin by enrolling in a puppy class or basic obedience course and following the directions of your instructor and those found in this book.

▼ Purchase some of the books and videos recommended in the Appendix.

▼ If the dog you acquired was not properly socialized during his formative first weeks, you will need to work extra hard to help mold his or her character.

Group Training Classes

Dog training is a learned skill, both mental and physical. The quickest way to learn is to participate in a class. Books, videos, and CDs can give you a taste of what's in store, but only a trainer can help you adjust your skills so that your dog understands and executes the various exercises you have asked him or her to perform.

Another benefit of group class training is that your dog has to learn to execute the commands in a setting that is distracting. It is easier to execute a command when it's just the two of you in a quiet setting. Performing the same exercise in a group takes the training to a whole different level.

The best way to find a trainer is to visit a session or two to see what you think of the trainer and his or her methods. While you are there, observe the facilities, the participants, and the dogs. Listen to what participants have to say to one another before and after class. Observe how the dogs behave. Before making a final decision, I suggest you visit at least one or two trainers.

To find a class, check with your veterinarian, look in the phone book, call your animal shelter or humane society, check with your city's parks and recreation department, call the schools and colleges, and check out the bulletin board listings at the pet supply stores.

Attending a group training session is only the beginning. What you learn there must be practiced at home. Your training sessions at home should be done on a daily basis. Keep them short and sweet—short, five to ten minutes, and sweet, use those treats!

Toys and Endearing Objects

Golden retrievers love to play with toys and carry things in their mouth. Because they are a retrieving breed, their natural instinct for holding something in their mouth is greater than it is for non-retrieving dogs. The following items are safe and enjoyable for golden retrievers.

▼ Tennis Balls
▼ Soft Bite toys (Teddy Bears and Dinosaurs)
▼ Kong Toys
▼ Knotted Towels
▼ Nylabones
▼ Toss/Floss Ropes
▼ Rawhide Chew Bones**
▼ Latex Porcupines
▼ Soft Frisbees/Flippy Flyers
▼ Large Fabric Balls
▼ Empty One-Gallon Plastic Milk Jugs (baby puppies only)
▼ Sterilized bones

Various toys
Courtesy of PetEdge

A word of caution! Never leave dogs or puppies alone to chew toys. When rawhide softens, it can break off and lodge in the throat, causing a dog to choke to death. I take the bones away after thirty minutes of constant chewing or when they become soft. The bone will harden again when left for twenty-four hours and can be given repeatedly until it is too small and you throw it away. Cow hooves have been known to splinter and can cause death. For this reason, I don't recommend their use.

> *Another word of caution!* Wash new tennis balls before giving them to your dog. Put them in the washing machine with detergent and run through a full cycle. Washing eliminates the excess dye that could be harmful.

Do not let your golden retrieve sticks or rocks. Purchase canvas or rubber training bumpers called "dummies." Tie a cord on the end, and you can throw them for long distances. You may also use tennis balls, soft Frisbees™, or the rubber balls with elastic bands. Hint: purchase an inexpensive tennis racquet for hitting the tennis balls. You get a lot of "bang" for your buck.

Just For Parents (and kids, too)

Introducing your new puppy to your household should be a happy event for all concerned. If very young children will be welcoming him or her, you must supervise the meeting and ALL subsequent interactions between your puppy and the children. Older children will also benefit from explanations about handling the new family member. Your puppy is bound to be apprehensive and unsure of how to handle all these new people and his or her new surroundings. Here are some basic rules to follow.

"Puppy Love"   *Photo: Mary Olson*

The Rules

▼ Young children must be taught to respect the puppy's well-being. Your puppy needs lots of rest, a regular schedule, and a place of comfort away from noise and constant movement. This is particularly critical during the first few weeks of life in his or her new home.

▼ Carefully introduce children to the puppy, teaching them to use slow movements and gentle handling. Young children must be taught to be kind to the puppy. The children may be apprehensive of the new puppy or may develop jealousies over the amount of attention the puppy is receiving. They should never be left unattended. Sharp jabs with a toy or a hefty poke from a child can injure the puppy and damage the relationship between the dog and the child.

▼ The puppy needs to learn where the children's place is in respect to the "pack" order. It is the adult's responsibility to guide and direct the puppy in understanding and making the decision that children are higher in the pack than the puppy itself.

How to Teach the Rules

1. First teach the puppy that you have the right to take his or her belongings (toys, food) away. He or she then will understand there is no threat in your removing these items. Puppies raised with their littermates become very protective of their toys and often make quite a game of keep away. They must learn not to feel threatened and not to play keep away with their human family.

   Grabbing and snatching a pup's toy is very different from gently teaching the puppy to give his or her toy upon command and then praising him or her for releasing it to you. It is your responsibility as an adult to teach the puppy to "give" his or her toy on command. After the puppy understands this command, your child may ask the puppy to "give" in the appropriate manner.

2. It is now time to teach your children to respect the puppy's toys. Since children do not like to have their toys snatched away by another, they will understand how the puppy feels. Explain to them the Golden Rule: "Do unto the puppy as you want done unto you." No snatching, grabbing, hitting!

Children should understand not to grab things away or tease the puppy by withholding its toys. Just as no child likes to have his toys snatched away by another, no puppy understands someone grabbing his toy when he is playing with it. Do not let your children play "tug of war" with a puppy.

The "Pack" Order

You can expect your puppy to place itself and the children into a "pack" order. Dogs are pack animals and will take their place in the pack according to age and status of the other "top dogs." The adult members of a human family are higher in the pack, with one being the "pack leader." The pack leader is generally the adult who feeds, walks, and spends the greatest amount of time with the dog.

A pup will decide a child's order in the pack by watching an adult's response to the child both with regard to the puppy and in general. If the puppy sees an adult condoning the child's behavior, he or she will be more accepting of the child. If the puppy observes an adult reprimanding the child, he or she may want to help. You will get this same response from your child when reprimanding the puppy. If you have to reprimand your child, try to do it out of the puppy's sight. Likewise, if you must reprimand the puppy, try not to have the child present. Use your parental discretion in this matter, as the age of the child and his or her ability to understand the process will determine the proper procedure.

If your child observes you reprimanding the puppy in an inappropriate manner, he or she will model his behavior after yours, and you have set yourself up for major problems with both puppy and child.

Without formal training, children should not be responsible for reprimanding the puppy. If the puppy resents the corrections and protests, the child is not equipped to give the correct response, and the puppy will be likely to take advantage of him or her.

When a dog is mauled, hurt, frightened, threatened, cornered, or suddenly startled, it may respond by biting. Some dogs have much better control of this reflex, but it is a normal response that can be controlled by teaching the puppy that biting is unacceptable. A child may create many such incidents without even realizing he or she is doing so. It is only prudent to teach children respect for the rights and well-being of the puppy. Children too young to fully understand should always be supervised when with the puppy.

Some Other Basic Rules

▼ **Teach children not to run and scream around the puppy.** This will excite him and will most likely lead to dominant and even aggressive behavior. Remember the puppy was raised in a pack; running, chasing, and growling with other puppies was how they determined their pack order.

▼ **Never tie your dog in the yard.** Children tend to tease tethered dogs even without realizing it, which can lead to aggressive behavior. Many instances of dogs attacking children occur when the dog is tethered in the yard and a screaming or running child enters its space.

▼ **Do not play tug-of-war** with your golden if he has access to children. A dog that learns to tug on any item will think that anything he can grab is his, even if it's a child's toy, clothing, or body part.

▼ **Make sure your dog is safe from harassment.** Children and immature adults often goad dogs to bark and snarl. They may also throw objects at the dog or get him to run the fence in an attempt to get at the person. Whatever the case, the end result will be the dog will learn to hate kids and some adults. This hatred may manifest itself as fear or as aggression and may result in a person being bitten and the dog being taken to the pound to be placed in a new home or euthanized.

▼ DO NOT **leave children under five unattended with a dog!** A young child may challenge or injure the dog unintentionally, and the result could be tragic. Dogs and children should be separated at snack time so the dog doesn't learn to steal food from tiny hands. I'll never forget an incident that occurred when I was about twelve years old. My neighbors had a beautiful Irish setter and a toddler. The toddler was playing with a set of keys (the real thing—metal) and, as toddlers are wont to do, looked for a place to put the keys. Yes, you guessed it, the keys ended up in the dog's rectum. Thankfully the dog was kind, and the child was not bitten. The dog recovered, and life went on as usual.

Right: Belle and Magic
Photo: Natalie Bailey

Below: Best Friends
Photo: Brandye Randermann

Just For Kids (and parents, too)

It Is Very Important to Know What Humane Means

Humane means acting kind, gentle, and generous toward your pet. Your new puppy needs to feel safe at all times. You can help him or her to feel that way by being humane to him or her. To help you remember what it means to be humane, you can sign the contract "How To Love Your Dog" at the end of this chapter and put it in your room.

Now that you understand the word humane, let's get your house ready for your new dog. Puppies are like babies—they get into lots of things that could hurt them, and they are very curious. Begin by puppy proofing your house to keep your new dog safe from danger.

Puppy Proof Your House

▼ Make sure cords and wires are not where your dog can reach them.

▼ Place trash in cupboards or have your parents get trashcans with lids.

▼ Ask your folks to remove dangerous liquids, like cleaners and antifreeze.

▼ Clear off tables that your pup might reach.

Puppy's First Day At Home

Give your dog a head start on a happy life by making his first day a great one. Your puppy's first day in your home is one of the most important times in his young life. Try to make it one of his best days.

It's very important for your dog to be wearing an ID tag from the first day he is at your home. Before you bring your new dog or puppy home, have the tag ready for him. If you haven't chosen a name for your dog yet, just put your address and phone number on the tag.

Starducks Macallen and Big Bird   *Photo: Ginger Garrett*

The first thing you are going to want to do is hold your puppy. You might want to hold him all the time. But it is very important for your puppy to have a chance to meet the other people in your family. He also needs to explore his new home. Holding your puppy is important so he learns to love you, but on the first day, hold him only a few minutes at a time.

Have a couple of toys ready for your dog to play with. He may not want to play the first day, but they'll be there when he wants them.

Have a place for your dog to sleep. A crate makes a good bed. When your puppy is resting, he can be in a private place where no one will bother him. If you don't have a crate, put his bed somewhere that is cozy, comfortable, and private for him.

Your pup will probably need to go to the bathroom soon after he arrives. It would be a good idea to take him outside before he begins to explore your home. Praise him when he goes.

Give your new dog time to explore your house, but don't leave him alone. You can stand behind him and follow him to the places he wants to go.

Quiet Please!

Your puppy will do better if your house is quiet. Loud noises may scare him. Later, when he is used to your house, you can introduce new sounds slowly.

Meeting Your Other Dog

The best place for your new dog to meet your other dog for the first time is outside—in your fenced yard. When they are comfortable with each other, bring them indoors together.

Time to Eat?

Wait and give your dog some food after he has been home for a while and is feeling more comfortable. Don't forget to let him outside every time he drinks or eats.

Training Tips

Don't start any training on this first day. This is your pup's day to meet everyone.

It might be very tempting to take your dog out and show her off to your friends, but you need to wait a little while. First, let your puppy get comfortable with her new home and with everyone that lives in your house. Then, after your puppy has had its shots to protect her from illness, take her out for short walks not very far from your house. Always remember to tell your puppy she is doing a great job.

Here are some simple hints on training. If you don't feel comfortable trying them, have your parents read this and watch them as they train the puppy. When you are ready, you can walk your dog, too!

Going for a Walk

Dogs love to go for walks, but they don't want to be pulled and tugged. Teaching your dog how to walk without pulling will help both of you to enjoy your time together.

Walking on a Leash

First, you need a four-foot leash and a nylon collar that won't slip off. DO NOT use a "choke" collar.

Leash training for puppies

▼ Start by attaching a lightweight leash to your puppy's collar.

▼ Drop the leash, and let the puppy drag it around.

▼ Call your puppy, tell her "good girl" and pet her.

▼ Leave the leash on for only a few minutes, and never leave it on her when you are not with her.

▼ Do this several times over a few days, and pretty soon your pup won't even notice the leash.

Start by having your dog sit on your left side, facing front just like you. As you say "Let's go," take a step starting with your left foot. Using your left foot all of the time will signal your dog that you are about to walk.

Walk at your normal walking pace, and talk to your dog while you walk. Tell her what a good girl she is. You want her to be happy walking with you. Keep talking to her. Make it fun.

Go a few feet, then stop. You can praise her now. Or you can have her sit and then praise her, as long as she stays with you.

If your dog is interested in everything around her except you, try getting her attention using her favorite treat. If there are too many distractions where you are, find a quiet place to start your training where your dog can concentrate on you.

Teaching "Be Gentle"

"Be gentle" is a very important command. It teaches your dog to take things from you gently, without grabbing or being rough. Your dog will be less likely to grab things from other people when she learns to be gentle, especially if other members in your family practice it, too.

This command is helpful when you give your dog a bone to eat or play with. It helps when you are giving her anything that she might put into her mouth. When your dog learns to be gentle, she becomes a much better pet. She learns to respect you as her leader and friend.

You can say, "Gentle," or "Easy," if you prefer. With a command like, "Be gentle," it is best to plan your teaching session. This means that you decide when you are going to teach it to your dog.

You should teach, "Be gentle," soon after a meal, so that your dog is not very hungry. Be careful not to *tease* your dog with this lesson. Always give her the treat as soon as she is being gentle. Then take a break and praise her in other ways such as playing fetch or hugging and kissing.

▼ Get a dog treat that your dog likes. Take the treat and your dog to a quiet place where you won't be disturbed. You and your dog need to be very calm. If your dog is not calm, wait until another time to teach this lesson.

▼ Because your dog may be impatient for the treat, ask her to sit or have someone hold her.

▼ Hold the treat in the palm of your hand, and while saying the words, "Be gentle," move the treat closer to your dog's mouth. Say the word calmly and slowly like "b-e-e g—e—n—t—l—e."

▼ If your dog starts to reach for the food, pull your hand away and say, "No-oo-" very softly. This should be a very calm time.

▼ Since you will be pulling your hand away when your dog grabs, she should stop trying to grab. Keep bringing your hand toward her mouth, and if she is being very gentle and not grabbing at all, let her take the treat.

Try this a couple of times a day for short periods of time, and before you know it people will be amazed at your incredible, non-grabbing dog!

Don't forget to go to the web site: www.loveyourdog.com for more training hints.

How To Love Your Dog

I, _____ , *promise to take care of my dog,* _____ , *during his/her whole lifetime. I will teach my dog to trust me by treating him/her with love and respect. I will be kind, gentle, and generous to my dog at all times. I will be responsible for providing him/her with the things that he/she needs to be healthy and happy. I am making this commitment to my dog.*

♡ *I will give food and water to my dog in a clean dish everyday.*

♡ *I will make sure my dog has shelter from hot, cold, and wet weather.*

♡ *I will make sure my dog sees a veterinarian for shots and checkups.*

♡ *I will provide a collar and ID tag for my dog to wear at all times.*

♡ *I will keep my dog from running loose in the neighborhood.*

♡ *I will make sure my dog gets obedience training so he or she behaves well.*

♡ *I will keep my dog clean and brushed and lookin' good!*

♡ *I will spend time everyday with my dog playing or going for a walk.*

♡ *I will always protect my dog from people or things that might hurt him or her.*

Your Signature_____

Reprinted with permission of Jan Wall
www.loveyourdog.com

Bringing Home Your Newly Adopted Rescue Golden Retriever

This section is reprinted with permission of Chesapeake Rescue.

CONGRATULATIONS!!! I'm so happy that you chose to help a GOLDEN in need and were willing to open your home and heart to help your new best friend.

The theme of this chapter is "**SET YOUR DOG UP TO SUCCEED!**" By understanding your new dog's behavior, you can anticipate problems and correct them calmly and as quickly as possible. Be reasonable in your expectations. Everyone concerned with the adoption of your golden wants this to be a "win-win" situation!

Before You Pick Up Your New Golden Retriever

Since you've chosen to adopt a golden retriever, you've probably educated yourself about the temperament, size, and natural instincts that make up the sporting breed known as golden retrievers. You are aware of the changes to your current lifestyle that this golden will cause (time set aside daily for exercise and work), and you're willing to accept full responsibility for this new member of your family.

Charger and his beloved tennis ball

Photo: Tracy Stevens

The adoption coordinator that you worked with told you about your golden's history, veterinary information, evaluations, and current eating, sleeping, and activity routines so that his or her transition into your home can be easier. Dogs need order and are extremely routine oriented. We recommend that you find out all you can about his or her routine—and duplicate what you can—*before* you start to reorient him or her to the rhythms and schedules of your home. Work out your *house rules* and dog-care regimen in advance among the human members of your household. Who will walk the dog first thing in the morning? Who will feed him or her at night? Will he or she be allowed on the couch or bed? Where will he or she sleep at night? Will he or she be crated?

To ensure a smooth transition, it is best if you purchase ahead of time the supplies (collar, ID tag, leash, food, bowls, crate, and toys) for your new dog.

Try and arrange the arrival of your new dog for a weekend—or when you can be home for a few days—for *quality, hands-on time.*

If you have *other pets,* make sure they are up to date on their shots and in general good health before bringing home your new dog. Despite the best efforts of the rescue organization, previous owner, or foster family, viruses can be spread and occasionally go home with adopted rescue dogs. You may wish to set up an appointment with your own vet to check out your new dog and set up an inoculation schedule, depending on the veterinary care your rescue dog has received.

Register for an *obedience class.* Don't ignore this very important step in setting up yourself and your rescued golden for success! Be dogged about finding an obedience class or trainer. There are many positive-reinforcement-based dog obedience classes that teach dog manners, canine good citizenship, and discipline. Try to register for a class starting about three to four weeks *after* your dog has come home with you. It is important that your new dog has some time to adjust to you and your home *before* putting him or her into the stimulating environment of an obedience class. Even the shortest "dog manners" course offered at your vet's will reinforce the new bond between you and your new golden, will give you a valuable face-to-face resource for questions about your dog's behavior, and will provide a powerful tool for moderating your rescue dog's less attractive behavior traits! Remember, goldens need work—this is a really easy way to provide him or her with active, mental work of which you'll approve! The rewards are obvious—what a joy it is to have a well-mannered, trained golden companion!

New families often ask about *changing the adopted dog's name*. If you desire to, it is fine. Many times, the dogs are given names at random by a shelter. The dog will learn his or her new name if it's overused in the beginning. It is in no way traumatic to the dog to change his or her name.

When You Arrive Home

You should expect your new dog to act differently than how she did when you met her at the foster/owner's home. She will be excited, nervous, and maybe tired after the trip to your house. Being routine oriented, your golden may have just gotten comfortable at her foster home; now she recognizes that the routine is changing yet again. She doesn't know the smells, the sounds, and, importantly, the routines and rules of your house. This is very confusing for her.

Dogs display *anxiety and nervousness* by panting, pacing, lack of eye contact, "not listening," housebreaking accidents, excessive chewing, gastric upset (vomiting, diarrhea, loose stools), crying, whining, jumpiness, and barking. This is a litany of behaviors any and every dog owner dreads! As long as you understand where these behaviors originate, you can perhaps address them *before* they appear and deal effectively with them when they do! Your goal in the next few weeks is to reduce the "noise and confusion in her head" and to get her to relax, to be calm, and to recognize how to be good. Despite your joy at adopting this golden (and after a few enthusiastic hugs and kisses), you should be calm, gentle, and firm with your dog. Talk to her in a calm, low voice as you travel home. Avoid playing the car radio and having too many people with you when you pick her up.

All rescue dogs go through a "honeymoon period." After the first day or so, the dog may be very quiet and extraordinarily controlled and "good." The "real" dog appears two to four weeks later—after she's mostly figured out the house rules, the schedule of the days, and the characters of her new family. At this time, she'll start testing out her position in the pack and may "regress" to puppyhood behaviors and "bad" behavior. Be patient with her and firm in your expectations. Praise her for appropriate behavior—especially when she is lying quietly and behaving herself. Don't constantly praise for nothing—the dog will learn to tune out your praise over time!

Things to Do

When you first bring your new dog home, make sure you have him on a leash!

Spend the first fifteen to thirty minutes walking him outside around the perimeter of your yard or the area where you will be with him most on your property. Walk slowly. Let him "lead" mostly, and let him sniff and pause if he wants to. He is getting used to the "lay of the land" and all the smells associated with his new home. He will undoubtedly relieve himself—this is his way of making himself at home by adding his mark to the smells of your home, now his new home. Obviously you want this to happen outside! If you have a place you wish this to happen, encourage him to "get busy" in that area, and praise him warmly when he does. The excitement of the move and new family will cause him to have to *relieve himself more often than normal.* You must be prepared to give him plenty of opportunities to do this in the beginning! Whenever the rescue dog is not confined, supervise him. Set this dog up to win!

You might want to consider isolating the new dog from your resident dogs during the first entry to your home. He will appreciate the safety and quiet as he explores your home. Crate your resident dog or have someone take him for a walk while your new dog explores.

Let the new dog explore the house. Leave him on leash, and make sure he's supervised AT ALL TIMES! We recommend leaving your new dog on leash in the house for the first day. Don't even leave the dog unsupervised while you answer the phone!

Once inside your house, a male may still accidentally mark a door, plant, or chair when he first walks inside your home. This is out of nervousness (or he may smell another dog), so it is best to leave him on the leash indoors the first day. If he starts to lift his leg, give him a short jerk on the leash, and tell him "No." That should stop him immediately and remind him of his housebreaking manners. Follow up this correction by taking him outside in case he's not just marking! Bear in mind that if your golden has a few accidents, it does not necessarily mean that he is not housebroken. We can't emphasize enough how much nerves and excitement can cause *uncharacteristic accidents*. Watch for typical pre-piddling behavior—circling, sniffing, etc. Do not scold or hit a dog for having an accident. Rather, verbally get his attention, grab the leash, and take him right outside to his spot to do his business. If he does it, praise him! Once he relaxes and learns the rhythms and routines of your home, all his manners will return!

Even when you're in a fenced yard, you'll want to leave your rescued golden on leash for the first week or so. This way, you can reinforce a recall command and help monitor pack behavior if you have other dogs. Until your new dog bonds to you and makes good eye contact, we recommend leaving him on leash.

Provide Quiet Time

Quiet time will be important for your new golden in the first week. Because of her nervousness and anxiety, she will get worn out fast. Her recent past may include a shelter stay that has worn her out with worry. Despite your excitement, try and resist

A big soft bed goes a long way to comfort a newly rescued retriever.

inviting friends and relatives over to visit your dog. Give her time to get used to your immediate family and resident pets only. If the dog does not solicit play or attention from you, let her alone to sleep or establish herself. Believe it or not, it's best not to force her to play at first!

Feed Your New Dog

Feed your new dog twice a day, half in the morning, half at night. Ask and encourage the dog to sit before putting the bowl down. Put the food bowl down for fifteen minutes. If the dog does not eat his food, pick up the bowl until the next mealtime. After a couple of days of this routine, even the most finicky of eaters will change their minds. By feeding this way, you can monitor exactly how much he is eating.

If you have *other dogs*, feed your rescue dog away from them but at the same time. You can feed in the same room, but use opposite corners, putting the dominant dog's bowl down first. This is usually the resident dog on the first few nights, but that situation may change over time! You may want to arrange to have another adult in the room for the first week of feedings to monitor the "pack behavior." Watch that each dog sticks to his own bowl. Keep vigilant over feeding time for a couple of months until the pack positions are worked out.

Consider Crating Your Dog

Many of the golden retrievers that pass through rescue have been crate trained at one time or another. Every dog needs a place to which to escape, a place to call her own, and a crate provides an answer to these needs! Your new golden will have some degree of separation anxiety when you leave her for work or alone at home. Crating the dog in the beginning will eliminate accidents, chewing destruction, and other mischievous activity that is rooted in nervousness and insecurity. Your dog is safest in the crate when you are not home until you can totally trust her loose in the house. This is especially true if you have resident pets, because you can't supervise their interactions when you're away or asleep!

Children should be taught to leave the dog alone if she retreats to her crate. You should never use the crate for disciplining. The crate must be a dog's sanctuary for crate training to be effective. Later, crates are great for traveling with your dog. She will always have a familiar den to which to retreat and feel comfortable and reassured.

Each time your dog is confined, make sure the dog knows she's a good dog. If your new golden is particularly emotional or anxious, try making good-byes and hellos as unemotional and nonchalant as possible.

While crating a dog helps make everybody safe, crating should NOT be abused by locking the dog in the crate all the time. Goldens need to be with you and should be with you unless they cannot be supervised or trusted alone in the house. For instance, if you are going to shower and the dog still sometimes chews, crate her for those fifteen minutes for safety, but then let her out to be with you. If the dog is crated while you are at work all day, you MUST make an extra effort to let the dog "hang" with you in the house until she is reliable loose on her own in the house.

If you prefer not to crate, make sure to set aside a safe, indestructible space in your home for your rescue dog. You may want to try using baby gates in the kitchen or hallway. Remember, you may really want to keep your dog on easy cleanup flooring at first!! If the area of confinement is too large, you may begin to have housebreaking accidents. We do not recommend the basement or garage, since your dog will not feel "part of the family" isolated away from it. If she can see and hear you, that is much better. This is why wire-style crates are so effective in the house.

Be Patient During the Honeymoon Period

There is a good chance that your rescued golden will show his insecurity by following you everywhere! This will include trying to hang with you in the bathroom, watching television with you, getting the mail, and undoubtedly wanting to sleep with you. It is not unusual for him to whine or cry or bark if confined away from you at night—lights out at a new strange place is a stressful thing for him. If you put the crate close to your bedroom or somewhere he can see you, the problems are usually minimized. Safe chew toys in the crate at night will give him something to do if he's awake. Remember, during the first couple of weeks, the dog will probably become quite tired and worn out by the day's activities, so establishing a sleep schedule is usually not a big deal. As you wean him from the crating at night, make sure he has been well exercised—a tired golden is usually a really good golden indoors!!

Establish a Routine

Try to develop *and use* a consistent daily routine for feeding, exercising, and bathroom duties. Dogs are creatures of habit and routine translates into security for them. If you do the same things, in the same way, and in the same order, she will settle in more quickly and learn what is expected of her and when.

Let your new golden out to air and take care of business as soon as you rise in the mornings. Feed her after a short walk or romp in the yard. Give her another chance to relieve herself before you go to work. Upon return from work, immediately let the dog out for exercise and a bathroom break. This is NOT the time to read the mail, make a phone call, or flop yourself on the sofa!!! If she's exercised heavily, wait thirty minutes or so before the evening feeding. She'll need another bathroom break anywhere from thirty minutes to several hours after the evening meal, depending on her age. It is your job to figure this out. She should get another airing right before you go to bed.

Socialize Your Rescued Golden

Rescue dogs come from a variety of backgrounds, but all dogs can do with more socialization. After your dog has time to settle into your home and is starting to look to you with confidence (within two to three weeks), start providing new socialization opportunities.

Now you can start inviting your friends and relatives over. Do introductions to new people gradually. Introductions can take the form of petting, playing fetch, even going for a walk. *Do not force the dog to accept new people.* Do it positively, with lots of praise, allowing the dog to approach people rather than new people approaching your dog! Be sure to tell your visitors that your dog has newly been rescued so they need to be more sensitive. Ask that they don't reach for the dog right away; let him come to them. If he does not go to the new person, that visitor should completely ignore the dog. Suggest that after the dog has met/sniffed the new person, they pat the side of the dog's neck or side of the shoulder instead. Patting a dog on the top of the head is interpreted by dogs as a powerful dominance attempt and can be a challenge to some dogs, a frightening thing to others.

Start taking your dog new places—nearby parks, dog-allowed beaches, and, especially to obedience classes! The opportunity will allow you to determine how your dog responds to strange people, dogs, and places.

This is an adage used by workers in GSD (German shepherd rescue). It is appropriate for rescued goldens, too.

> *Authority without domination.*
> *Love without subservience.*
> *Respect without fear.*

You do not need to frighten your dog into complying with household obedience commands or prove to him that you are the toughest creature around by using constant brute force. You DO need to show your dog that you are the leader in the household, a leader in whom he should put his trust. You can do this by "telling" your dog this in a language he understands—body language and daily habits. Respect is not something that you can force a creature into giving you.

Above all, be patient, firm, and consistent with your new golden. Use positive reinforcement and lots of praise when he's good. When he makes mistakes, correct him when it's happening, and praise him when he modifies his behavior. Undoubtedly you will get lots of advice—good and bad—from other dog owners! Read and research as much as you can to prepare yourself. Understand that sometimes you may need to try more than one approach to a problem because every golden is different.

Most rescue and adoption coordinators will follow up on the dogs they place. Most rescuers are backed up by dog behavior and health experts within their own local organization, so if they don't know the answer to a problem, they can ask others. Don't be afraid to ask questions or bring up new situations and feelings of frustration that you may experience! The goal of a rescue organization is to make sure rescue dogs never have to be uprooted again, so they are quite interested in helping you troubleshoot any problems—the sooner the better—before they become big problems that threaten the placement!

Love and Enjoy Your New Dog!

Most of all, be prepared to give and receive more love, affection, and loyalty than you ever thought possible! Enjoy your golden retriever for many years to come, and thanks again for helping rescue a golden!

Canine Good Citizen

What Is the Canine Good Citizen Program?

The Canine Good Citizen is a program developed by the American Kennel Club. For additional information see the web site: www.akc.org

The purpose of the Canine Good Citizen Test is to ensure that your dog is accepted as a respected member of the community because he has been trained and conditioned to "put his best foot forward" at home, in public, and in the presence of other dogs. The program embraces both purebred and mixed breed dogs, as the anti-canine sentiment does not discriminate between purebred dogs and the non-purebred.

Canine Good Citizen training is fun and useful. Through it, you and your dog will establish a closer bond, and your dog will have the added benefit of knowing how to please you. This test of your dog's manners and training is not a competition and does not require that you and your dog perform with precision.

The American Kennel Club urges all dog owners to participate in this program, thereby assuring that our beloved dogs will always be welcomed and respected members of the community. Here is the test.

Demonstrating confidence and control, the dog must complete these ten steps. *(Note: At check in, before beginning Test 1, the owner must present a current rabies certificate and any other state or locally required inoculation certificates and licenses.)*

Test 1: Accepting a Friendly Stranger

This test demonstrates that the dog will allow a friendly stranger to approach it and speak to the handler in a natural, everyday situation. The evaluator and handler shake hands and exchange pleasantries. The dog must show no sign of resentment or shyness and must not break position or try to go to the evaluator.

Test 2: Sitting Politely for Petting

This test demonstrates that the dog will allow a friendly stranger to touch it while it is out with its handler. With the dog sitting at the handler's side, the evaluator pets the dog on the head and body *only*, then circles the dog and handler, completing the test. The dog must not show shyness or resentment.

Test 3: Appearance and Grooming

This practical test demonstrates that the dog will welcome being groomed and examined and will permit a stranger, such as a veterinarian, dog groomer, or friend of the owner, to do so. It also demonstrates the owner's care, concern, and responsibility. The evaluator inspects the dog, then combs or brushes the dog and lightly examines the ears and each front foot.

Test 4: Out For a Walk (Walking on a Loose Leash)

This test demonstrates that the handler is in control of the dog. The dog may be on either side of the handler, whichever the handler prefers. There must be a left turn, a right turn and an about turn, with at least one stop in between and another at the end. The dog need not be perfectly aligned with the handler and need not sit when the handler stops.

Test 5: Walking Through a Crowd

This test demonstrates that the dog can move about politely in pedestrian traffic and is under control in public places. The dog and handler walk around and pass close to several people (at least three). The dog may show some interest in the strangers, without appearing overexuberant, shy, or resentful. The handler may talk to the dog and encourage or praise the dog throughout the test. The dog should not be straining at the leash.

Test 6: Sit and Down on Command/ Staying in Place

This test demonstrates that the dog has training, will respond to the handler's command to sit and down, and will remain in the place commanded by the handler (sit or down position, whichever the handler prefers). The handler may take a reasonable amount of time and use more than one command to make the dog sit and then down. When instructed by the evaluator, the handler tells the dog to stay and walks forward the length of a twenty-foot line. The dog must remain in place, but may change positions.

Test 7: Praise/Interaction

This test demonstrates that the dog can be easily calmed following play or praise and can leave the area of this test in a mannerly fashion. The handler may use verbal praise, petting, playing with a toy, and/or a favorite trick, in the allowed ten seconds of play, and then must calm the dog for the next test.

Test 8: Reaction to Another Dog

This test demonstrates that the dog can behave politely around other dogs. Two handlers and their dogs approach each other from a distance of about ten yards, stop, shake hands and exchange pleasantries, and continue on for about five yards. The dogs should show no more than a casual interest in each other.

Test 9: Reactions to Distractions

This test demonstrates that the dog is confident at all times when faced with common distracting situations, such as the dropping of a large book or a jogger running in front of the dog. The dog may express a natural interest and curiosity and may appear slightly startled, but should not panic, try to run away, show aggressiveness, or bark.

Test 10: Supervised Isolation

This test demonstrates that a dog can be left alone, if necessary, and will maintain its training and good manners. Evaluators are encouraged to say something like, "Would you like me to watch your dog while you make your call?" to add a touch of reality and accentuate the fact that leaving a dog tied and unsupervised is not condoned. The dog will be attached to a six-foot line for three minutes and does not have to stay in position, but should not continually bark, whine, howl, pace unnecessarily, or show anything other than mild agitation or nervousness.

Do I have to take the test?

No, but taking and passing the test will affirm your dog's right to earn the certificate issued by the American Kennel Club. Your dog will receive a certificate and be recorded with the AKC as a Canine Good Citizen. You may also use the suffix CGC after your dog's registered name. If you don't want to take the test, but have progressed through all these exercises, you will have assured yourself that your dog is a Canine Good Citizen.

Chapter 8

Maintaining Your Golden Retriever's Health

Maintaining your dog's health is critical to his overall well-being. In this section you will learn the importance of feeding a high-quality diet, how to keep your dog free of parasites and fleas, and how to remove a tick.

▼ Feeding Your Golden
▼ Vaccinations
▼ Flea Control
▼ Internal Parasites
▼ Lyme Disease
▼ Removing Ticks

Feeding Your Golden Retriever

There is no substitute for a balanced diet, however, with hundreds of brands to choose from, how do you know which one is best for your dog? The question most people ask is "does it really matter?" The answer is YES, it does matter. Different breeds flourish on different diets. Based on my own studies and experience feeding different breeds for more than thirty years, I know that it is simply not possible for one food to meet the needs of all dogs. Armed with that knowledge, I'm going to give you my personal opinion with respect to feeding a golden retriever.

Over the years, I've fed a number of brands—all high-quality premium feeds—and I've also prepared and fed a couple of the raw food diets. If you are interested in learning more about the raw food diets, refer to the Appendix for web sites and books.

What to Feed?

Follow your breeder's recommendation. If your puppy is thriving, continue with the program. If not, discuss the problem with your breeder.

My Current Feeding Program

▼ Weaning, six to nine weeks—Eukanuba Small Breed Puppy
▼ Nine weeks to one year—Eukanuba Large Breed Puppy
▼ One year through Adult—Eukanuba Adult Large Breed

A golden puppy will eat three meals a day until he is about twelve weeks of age. At that time you can divide his meals into two feedings per day. If you can't find someone to feed him a noon meal, divide his feedings into two. A golden should *always* be fed two meals a day. Feeding less (1) may cause bloating and/or indigestion.

Hey, I'm hungry!

Photo: Ginger Garrett

I use additives very sparingly. I give puppies and older dogs Vitamin C. I also supplement my older dogs (eight years and up) with a glucosomine/chronditin supplement. Dogs that are being campaigned, used actively for hunting or whelping, or subjected to extra stress receive a supplement such as Missing Link and may receive MSM and antioxidants.

I have fed my goldens the following commercial feeds with good results: Eukanuba, Nutro-Natural Plus, Sensible Choice Large Breed Puppy, Purina Pro Plan-Turkey/Barley, Solid Gold Hunchen Flocken.

How Much Should You Feed?

Here is a general guideline on the amount of feed your golden retriever puppy will consume. A male adult will generally maintain good weight—with moderate exercise—on four cups per day. A bitch will generally maintain on three cups per day. Older dogs need less food and should be fed a diet formulated for older dogs.

▼ Eight to ten weeks of age—½ to ¾ cup—three times daily
▼ Ten to twelve weeks of age—1 to 1½ cups—two times daily
▼ Twelve to sixteen weeks of age—2 cups—two times daily
▼ Six to twelve months—2 to 2½ cups—two times daily

Quite often, young dogs between the ages of *nine and fourteen months* will require extraordinary amounts of feed. They may consume up to seven cups per day. This is a time when they are growing at a rapid rate both internally and externally. Use your hands and eyes to determine the amount your dog requires. If you can feel (not see) your dogs ribs covered with a thin layer of fat, he is at perfect weight. If a dog is working, showing, hunting, etc., you may have to increase the feed. During the winter, if your dog is outside for long periods of time, you will need to feed more.

Feeding Schedule

Maintain the same time schedule for feeding seven days per week. This will help establish a pattern and aid in house training. Scientific evidence shows that pups will grow to their genetic potential eventually, despite a slow start at birth. As long as they gain evenly and slowly from birth they will attain maximum growth.

Supplements

Though conclusive studies are not yet complete, there is evidence that Vitamin C aids in reducing the incidence of hip dysplasia. It also acts as an aid to the immune system. You may begin to supplement with 500 mg. Vitamin C immediately. There are a variety of brands available in tablet or powder. I recommend using the timed-release caplets with rose hips. The caplets may be put in with the dog's feed and will be eaten with the food. The powdered form may also be used. When your puppy is four months old, increase the dosage to 1,000 mg. At ten months, increase to 1,500 mg., and between ten months and twenty-four months, feed 2,000 mg. per day. Divide the dosage into two tablets. Simply add to the dog's feed and moisten with hot water. If your dog's stools become loose, reduce the amount of Vitamin C until they are firm and continue with that dosage.

Vaccinating Your Puppy

There is no questioning the importance of an adequate vaccination program for the prevention of disease in puppies. Puppies receive temporary immunity from mothers that have been vaccinated for these diseases, but in order to continue protection as the immunity from the mother decreases, it is necessary to begin a vaccination program.

During the last several years, there has been a great deal of discussion and controversy in the veterinary medical field with regard to the efficacy and protocols of canine vaccinations Many traditional veterinarians have modified their vaccination protocols based on these findings.

My own vaccine protocol has changed as well. I am not a veterinarian and will not make a specific recommendation because I believe that you need to follow the advice of your own veterinarian. This is what my current veterinarian recommends.

 ▼ Six weeks: Parvo/Measles vaccine
 ▼ Eight weeks: Parvo/Measles vaccine
 ▼ Ten weeks: DHPPC and Bordetella
 ▼ Five to six months: Rabies
 ▼ Six months: Heartworm Test - begin monthly heartworm treatment with Interceptor

My veterinarian does not vaccinate with any vaccine containing leptosporosis.

Bordetella is a vaccine that provides immunity for several different viruses more commonly known as "kennel cough." If you are traveling with your dog, visiting lots of parks or venues where a large number of dogs congregate, you may want to consider the Bordetella vaccine. If you are planning on boarding your dog at a "boarding kennel" or veterinarian, you will be required to have a current Bordetella vaccination.

In areas where heartworm is prevalent, discuss with your veterinarian the use of heartworm medication. This medication is available as a once-a-month pill. There are also six-month injections available.

The information in this section is not given as medical advice. You are advised to seek the medical advice of a licensed veterinarian. Most veterinarians have "puppy packages," which include a total series of puppy vaccinations plus fecal examinations to detect worms. Here is an example of one of my veterinarian's puppy packages.

▼ All vaccinations six weeks to twelve weeks
▼ (2) Fecal analysis
▼ Worming medication as indicated by fecal analysis
▼ Rabies vaccination at five to six months
▼ Heartworm Test—six months
▼ Six-month supply of heartworm medication

The cost of a puppy package will vary depending upon the city and/or state in which you live. You may also purchase a puppy package that includes spaying or neutering. Puppy packages generally reflect quite a savings, so be sure to ask. Be prepared to pay the full amount in advance. The puppy package is an agreement between you and your veterinarian. He provides the services at a discount, and you agree to bring your puppy in for the full series.

> **CAUTION**: Until your puppy has had at least three vaccinations, do not take him to public places frequented by other dogs that may not be vaccinated. To do so may result in severe illness and/or death.

Flea Control

Everyone is looking for magic in solving the perennial problem of fleas. Although there is no magic available, there are certain prescribed methods that are effective in eliminating the pesky flea.

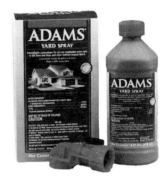

Adams Flea Spray
Photo courtesy of PetEdge

Topical products such as Advantage, Advantage Plus, Frontline, Frontline Plus, etc., are very effective in killing fleas and eggs. The "plus" products are also advertised as effective for killing ticks. These products are applied topically by squeezing the small applicator tip onto an area along the top of the dog's neck. The Advantage brand is absorbed into the first layer of the skin, and Frontline is absorbed into the base of each hair follicle.

There are also several flea pills on the market. Program, a once-a-month flea pill, acts as flea birth control. In other words, it inhibits fleas from reproducing. Sentinel is a once-a-month pill combining flea control and heartworm medication. In areas where fleas are a persistent and difficult problem, you may want to use both a topical and the pill. The pill doesn't kill fleas, but it does prohibit eggs from hatching and creating more fleas. Thus the vicious cycle is broken.

All of these products are available from a veterinarian. Discuss with your veterinarian which products are best suited for your area.

Where to Begin

1. Shampoo and dry your dog.

2. Apply topical flea product such as Advantage or Frontline.

3. Treat the outdoor environment using a compatible spray made especially for outdoor use. If you cannot treat the whole area because of its size, then treat the area in which the dog spends most of his time. Repeat this process monthly during peak flea season.

4. Treat the indoor environment, first by cleaning and vacuuming. Putting a flea collar in the vacuum bag will help in removing fleas. Vacuum your home two or three times weekly. Choose a compatible fogger or hand-held sprayer (same brand as you use on the dog and outside) to treat carpets, furniture, dogs' bedding, and vehicles in which the dogs travel.

The required number and size of foggers can be confusing if the exact square footage of areas to be covered is not known. As a rule of thumb, one six-ounce fogger per bedroom is recommended and a twelve-ounce fogger for the living room, dining room, and family room. Also, don't forget to treat the garage.

Flea Busters is a company that will treat the inside of your home with a product that is safe for humans and animals. They guarantee that your home will remain flea free for one year. This service only works if you have carpeting, as the company treats the carpet and furniture.

No single product can eradicate a flea infestation problem. Flea resistance can occur with constant exposure to one product over time, so switching brands and substances every so often is recommended. Whatever you use, avoid potential toxicity to yourself and your animals; read the label carefully and follow directions.

Fleas transmit several viral and bacterial diseases and are the intermediate host for tapeworms. Fleas and flea products can also cause allergic reactions in certain hypersensitive dogs. If you suspect your dog of being allergic to any product, consult your veterinarian immediately.

Flea Facts

▼ It is possible for fleas to produce a new generation every three weeks.

▼ Fleas don't live at altitudes higher than 5,000 feet and cold temperatures can kill them.

▼ Fleas lay more eggs when temperatures reach the range of 65 degrees F to 80 degrees F.

▼ Adult fleas separated from the host live one to two months.

▼ Mating and reproduction take place when the adult flea finds a host.

▼ A female flea will lay between four hundred and five hundred eggs in her lifetime.

▼ Eggs may be deposited on or off the dogs. The eggs hatch within seven to ten days.

▼ Adult fleas represent only one percent of the problem. The remaining ninety-nine percent is in the egg, larvae, or pupae.

▼ In thirty days, ten fleas can multiply to a quarter million.

Questions and Answers About Internal Parasites

Question: What are worms?

Answer: Worms are an internal parasite. All dogs are susceptible to several very common internal parasites that most of us refer to as "worms." In addition to worms, there are other common internal parasites, called protozoa, that may also infest your dog. Nearly all dogs get worms, so it is important that you have your veterinarian periodically check your dog's feces for parasites. This procedure is called a "fecal analysis," and it is a very inexpensive way to see if your dog is infested with "worms." It is important to know what type of parasite is present because there are several different types of wormers that treat various parasitic infestations.

Question: Do internal parasites pose a health hazard for my family?

Answer: Occasionally, under conditions of poor hygiene, some worms and protozoa can be transmitted to your family. This is of particular concern with young children who can contract roundworms or hookworms by placing their fingers in their mouth after playing outdoors in grass or soil that has been contaminated with these eggs. Also of concern are the protozoa Giardia, which can be contracted by drinking contaminated water, usually while on a camping or hiking trip.

Question: How can I tell if my dog has internal parasites?

Answer: In most cases, you cannot tell that your dog has an internal parasite problem until it becomes overwhelmed by the infestation. When this happens, you may notice poor appetite, coughing, vomiting, diarrhea, anemia, weight loss, potbelly, a rough dry coat, and an overall rundown appearance. Licking the anal region and/or dragging the rear end can also be an indication of an intestinal parasite infestation. However, scooting on the rear end can also mean that your dog's anal sacs (located on either side of the anal opening) have become plugged or infected.

Common Worms and Protoza Affecting Golden Retrievers

Roundworms

Look like white spaghetti noodles. Nearly all puppies have roundworms and must be treated beginning at two to three weeks of age and every ten to fourteen days until tested clear.

Tapeworms

Tapeworms are white, segmented, flat, and ribbon--like in appearance. They can be up to twenty inches in length. You may see tapeworm segments in your pet's stool or clinging to the hair near the tail. They look like small pieces of rice. They are commonly found in dogs. Infestation with tapeworms normally occurs when your dog eats fleas. Fleas are the most frequent transmission because they are so abundant in the pet and rodent population. They can also be ingested if your dog eats raw meat. The treatment for tapeworms is different than that used for roundworms. Treat immediately if you see those "little rice-looking pieces." A fecal analysis will also indicate the existence of tapeworm.

Hookworms
: Are tiny, thread-like bloodsucking parasites with razor-sharp mouth parts that pierce your dog's small intestine resulting in tissue damage, bloody diarrhea, and anemia. They are voracious feeders. Hookworm larvae are introduced when eggs are deposited in the stool of infected animals and they contaminate the soil. The hookworm larvae penetrate your dog's skin and enter into the blood system where they make their way to the lungs. They are then coughed up to the trachea and swallowed, where they proceed to the small intestine and eventually mature. Nearly all puppies have hookworms and must be treated beginning at two to three weeks of age. Multi-purpose wormers typically treat roundworms and hookworms.

Heartworms
: Dogs are the primary species affected by heartworms. They are a serious health threat to your dog ultimately resulting in heart failure and death. PREVENTION is the key as treating an advanced infection is expensive, complex, and dangerous. Treatment is not always successful, and some dogs may die from treatment complications.

Question: What are the symptoms of heartworms?

Answer: Dogs do not have symptoms during the early stages of a heartworm infestation. They can easily be infected for a year without showing any signs of infection. By the time symptoms occur, the condition is well advanced and difficult to treat.

Question: Can my dog be tested for heartworms?

Answer: The only accurate way to determine if your pet has heartworms is to have your veterinarian take a blood sample from your dog and run a test. **All dogs must be tested from the age of six months. Giving medication to a dog with an existing case of heartworm can kill the dog.**

Question: If my dog has heartworms, how is it treated?

Answer: If the dog tests positive, the adult heartworms can be killed through a series of injections of a very potent drug.

Question: How can I prevent my dog from getting heartworms?

Answer: Prevention is simple and usually one hundred percent effective. Once your veterinarian has tested the dog and determines that it does NOT have an existing heartworm infection, your veterinarian will prescribe either a once-a-month medication or the six-month vaccine that destroys any immature heartworms that have been deposited into your pet's bloodstream from the bite of an infected mosquito.

Whipworms	Whipworms occur when your dog swallows whipworm eggs found in contaminated soil. Whipworms can cause watery, soft stools, which are sometimes streaked with blood. In heavier infestation, one will notice increased diarrhea with blood, weight loss, pain, and general ill health.
Coccidiosis	Coccidia are classified as protozoa, which are microscopic, single-celled organisms. Coccidia are more common in overcrowded environments and during the stress of weaning. Signs of coccidiosis infection are bloody diarrhea, listlessness, dehydration, and abdominal pain.
Giardia	Giardia are protozoa, which are microscopic single-celled organisms. Clinical signs of Giardia range from mild intestinal discomfort to a sudden onset of explosive diarrhea, which is sometimes bloody and accompanied by a foul-smelling gas. Both pets and humans can become infected by drinking contaminated water from streams and ponds. Dogs can also contract this infection by eating droppings of contaminated animals. *If your golden retriever displays any of the symptoms listed here, be sure to take him to a veterinarian for an examination and fecal test.*

Lyme Disease

Question: What is Lyme disease?

Answer: Lyme disease can be very debilitating. The disease is transmitted to humans and animals through certain species of ticks.

Question: Where is Lyme disease found?

Answer: Lyme disease appears in almost every state in the United States. First discovered in Connecticut in 1975, it is suspected that migratory birds have helped distribute infected ticks across the country. It has also been found in many other parts of the world, including Australia, Africa, and Asia. It takes only one bite from an infected tick to transmit the disease.

Question: How is Lyme disease transmitted?

Answer: Lyme disease can be transmitted after an infected tick attaches itself to the skin of its victim and begins to take a blood meal. The tick has to be attached to the victim for one to two days before a disease-causing dose can be delivered. Prompt and proper removal of the ticks from your pet may prevent the transmission.

Question: What are the symptoms of Lyme disease?

Answer: Early symptoms include a spreading roundish rash often accompanied by flu-like symptoms, fever, fatigue, joint and muscle aches, and sometimes loss of appetite. This rash or reddened area looks like a "target" or "bull's-eye" and can easily go unnoticed on your dog.

Question: Can Lyme disease be treated?

Answer: Yes, with early diagnosis and antibiotic therapy. Cure rates are not as readily seen if Lyme disease is diagnosed late in the course of the illness.

Question: Is there a vaccine available?

Answer: Yes. Depending on the area in which you live, it is best to discuss the advantages and/or disadvantages of vaccinating against Lyme disease.

How To Remove A Tick

Prompt removal of ticks will help prevent Lyme disease transmission. It is imperative that you thoroughly examine every area of your golden retriever's body if you have been hiking in the woods or traveling anywhere that ticks are prevalent. A tick's mouthparts have harpoon-like barbs; they do not screw into the skin.

▼ DO NOT crush, jerk, or twist the tick when you are removing it. Exposure to the tick's body fluids could lead to the transmission of Lyme disease.

▼ DO NOT use your fingers to remove the tick.

▼ Using tweezers or forceps, grasp the tick's mouthparts as close to the skin as possible.

▼ Gently pull the tick straight out, steadily and firmly.

▼ After removal, wash your hands and the "bite site" with soap and water, and apply an antiseptic to the "bite site."

Chapter 9

Handling Medical Emergencies

These pages contain information that is CRITICAL to your dog's well-being. Please pay particular attention to the Household Poisons and Poisonous Plants lists and make sure your dog does not have access to these items. Check with your veterinarian to see if he or she is a member of the new Veterinary Hotline with the Poison Control Center. This timesaving service offered to veterinarians could make the difference between life and death for your dog.

▼ Common Household Poisons
▼ Poisonous Plants
▼ Creating a First Aid Kit
▼ First Aid for Medical Emergencies
▼ First Aid for Common Medical Problems

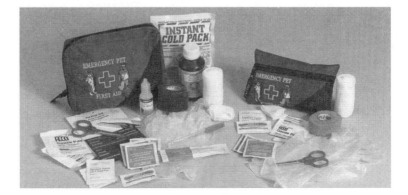

Common Household Poisons

Acetaminophen (Tylenol, Datril, etc.)
Antifreeze
Snail/
Bleach
Soaps
Lead
Brake Fluid
Tar
Matches
Carburetor Cleaner
Windshield
Mineral Spirits
Deodorants
Wood Preservatives
Nail Polish
Nail Polish Remover
Paint
Permanent Wave Lotion
Phenol
Photographic Developer
Paint
Gasoline
Hair Colorings
Herbicides

Kerosene
Slug Bait
Laxatives
Boric Acid
Suntan Lotion
Lye
Carbon Monoxide
Turpentine
Metal Polish
Cleaning Fluid
Washer Fluid
Moth Balls
Deodorizers
Detergents
Disinfectants
Drain Cleaner
Dye
Fungicides
Furniture Polish
Rat Poison
Rubbing Alcohol
Shoe Polish
Sleeping Pill

Courtesy of the American Humane Association

Creating a First Aid Kit

Like their human counterparts, dogs are subject to medical emergencies. In fact, many of the accidents or malfunctions that occur in the canine anatomy are similar to those that occur in the human body. There are, however, several critical differences, and medications that work wonders for humans can be lethal for our dogs.

Preparing a first aid kit for your dog and knowing when and how to use the various medications and equipment could save your dog's life. It will also help you to achieve peace of mind when an emergency arises. If your dog travels with you frequently, be sure to take the kit with you on each occasion. You

Common Plants that are Poisonous to Dogs

Amaryllis (bulb)	Elephant Ear	Monkshood
Andromeda	English Ivy	Mushrooms
Apple Seeds (cyanide)	Elderberry	Narcissus
Arrowgrass	Fox Glove	Nightshade
Avocado	Hemlock	Oleander
Azalea	Holly	Peach
Bittersweet	Hycinth (bulb)	Philodendron
Boxwood	Hydrangea	Poison Ivy
Buttercup	Iris (bulb)	Privet
Caladium	Japanese Yew	Rhododendron
Castor Bean	Jasmine (berries)	Rhubarb
Cherry Pits (cyanide)	Jerusalem Cherry	Snow on Mountain
Chokecherry	Jimson Weed	Stinging Nettle
Climbing Lilly	Laburnum	Toadstool
Crown of Thorns	Larkspur	Tobacco
Daffodil (bulb)	Laurel	Tulip (bulb)
Daphne	Locoweed	Walnut
Delphinium	Marigold	Wisteria

may find it easier to make a kit for home and one for the car. Many of the suppliers shown in the Appendix offer ready-made first aid kits, and you can add other items specifically designed to meet the needs of your dog. You can also make your own kit from the items shown below and add other items that have been recommended for your dog(s) by your veterinarian.

CAUTION—TOXIC—DO NOT USE

▼ Tylenol—Toxic to the liver

▼ Ibuprofen (Nuprin, Motrin, Advil, or any drug containing Ibuprofen) is extremely toxic and fatal to dogs even at low dosages

Safe for Use in Dogs

▼ Aspirin or Ascriptin (preferred)

Assemble the Kit

Purchase a plastic or rubber container with a secure lid, or use a tackle or toolbox; a large portable soft-sided cooler with handle also works well. Make sure the box is clearly marked indicating that it is a first aid kit for the dog.

Label the Kit (inside or out)

▼ Name, address, and phone number.

▼ Name and number of an emergency contact, someone that will take care of your pet if you are incapacitated.

▼ Name and phone number of your veterinarian.

▼ A signed statement from you, authorizing any veterinarian to treat your pet in case of an emergency.

▼ Provide a list of each pet's name, and list any medication he or she must take.

Medications

▼ Aspirin—as directed by veterinarian
▼ Benadryl—as directed by veterinarian
▼ Hydrocortisone Spray—consult your veterinarian
▼ Hydrogen peroxide to induce vomiting
*There are specific incidences where vomiting SHOULD NOT be induced. Talk with your veterinarian to obtain this information.
▼ Immodium—as directed by veterinarian
▼ Kaopectate—as directed by veterinarian
▼ Opti Clear—for eyes—consult your veterinarian
▼ Otomax—for ears, consult your veterinarian
▼ Panalog Ointment—consult your veterinarian
▼ Pepto Bismol Liquid or Pepto Bismol tablets—as directed by veterinarian

Supplies

▼ Antiseptic wipes
▼ Adhesive bandages
▼ Canine eye wash
▼ Canine thermometer (not human)

▼ Cotton gauze bandage
▼ Cotton gauze pads
▼ First aid tape
▼ Hot spot remedy
▼ Gold Bond powder (for quick treatment of hot spots)
▼ Allercaine anti-itch spray
▼ Hydrogen peroxide 3%
▼ Isopropyl rubbing alcohol
▼ Matches
▼ Muzzle (See section on Muzzle for instructions)
▼ New Skin Liquid Bandage
(good for emergency with torn pads on feet)
▼ Oral syringe
▼ Cotton-tipped swabs
▼ Safety pins in several sizes
▼ Small scissors with a blunt tip
▼ Snake bite kit—see your veterinarian

▼ Give liquid medications using an oral syringe tucked into the side of the dog's mouth, holding jaws closed.

▼ Over the counter medications—obtain correct dosage from your veterinarian. Generally one phone call will provide you with all the information you need to use these medications in their proper dosage for your dog.

Note: Review the contents of your first aid kit with your veterinarian.

The suggestions made by the author are based upon her knowledge and experience and should never be substituted for the advice of a licensed veterinarian. Consult your own veterinarian for the exact dosage and use of each medication for each dog. Study the labels and acquaint yourself with any side effects and how they might affect your particular pet. Although the recommended drugs are not prescription medications, there may be some dogs that will experience a severe reaction.

For detailed information on descriptions and information, refer to *Dog Owner's Home Veterinary Handbook,* by D. G. Carlson and J. M. Giffin, Howell Book House, and *The Merck Veterinary Manual,* published by Merck & Co., 1991.

Identification

Be sure your dogs travel with identification. Collars with their names and your phone number are important. When traveling with more than one dog, label your crates with the dogs' names. Attach the collar and leash to the front of the dog's crate. (I don't normally leave a collar on my dogs when they are crated. This prevents the collar or tags from hanging up on the crate.) You may choose to leave the collar on your dog, but do attach the leash to the front of the crate. In case of emergency, the collar and leash are readily available and can be snapped on in order to remove the dog from the car.

First Aid For Medical Emergencies

Muzzle

It is best to purchase a muzzle and keep it in your first aid kit. In case of emergency, where none is available, you can make one.

1. Make a closed loop with a half-knot and slip it over the dog's nose.

2. Make another closed loop with a half-knot and pull tightly so the half-knot is under the jaw.

3. Complete the muzzle by tying a tight bow behind the dog's ears.

Taking a Dog's Pulse

The femoral pulse, located on the inside of your dog's upper rear legs, is easy to monitor. Using any finger except your thumb, find the femur (the top bone in the rear leg) and then move a tiny distance forward. You should be able to feel the femoral artery pulsating. With practice, you'll find it quickly and recognize what feels normal. Get used to your dog's pulse strength and pulse rate. Next, place your free hand over the dog's heart and simultaneously feel the pulse and the heartbeat. A pulse in the leg should follow every beat of the heart. Inconsistencies are called arrhythmia's—skipped or dropped beats. Bear in mind that a dog's normal heartbeat speeds up a bit when it inhales and slows down when it exhales, but this should follow a regular pattern.

Bloat

Bloat occurs when air becomes trapped in the stomach, causing distention and discomfort. It is most common in very large breeds. It can occur in golden retrievers. Bloat can lead to gastric torsion, where the stomach twists on itself. Gastric torsion, if not treated quickly, *can be fatal.*

What Are the Early Signs of Bloat?

The most common is distress. The dog will be restless and won't sit down. If you know your dog well, the distress will be obvious in its expression and movements. Other signs include a painful back (the pain begins in the stomach, but the dog will react when you try to pet it), a rapid and weak pulse, and regurgitation. Regurgitation occurs in the esophagus and is different from vomiting in that the dog's stomach will not heave or contract. The dog may regurgitate some fluid, or simply air.

If you see any of these signs, have someone gently walk the dog while you call your veterinarian. Signs include an enlarged or rounded abdomen, lethargy, pale gums, and a dry mouth or nose. If you see any of these signs, get your dog to the vet *immediately.*

CPR

1. Place the dog on its side.

2. For small dogs, place your thumb on one side of the chest and your fingers on the other side. Compress the chest by squeezing. For large dogs, place both hands, one on top of the other, over the heart (where the point of the elbow meets the rib cage) and compress the chest by exerting downward pressure.

3. Chest compression must be rapid, about one hundred compressions per minute.

4. Stop every thirty seconds to determine if heartbeat has returned.

Choking and Artificial Respiration

1. Place dog on its side with its neck extended.

2. Open its mouth and inspect for food, vomit, etc.

3. Pull the tongue out carefully to avoid being bitten. This may reveal a foreign body over the back of the tongue.

4. Use long-nosed pliers or, if the dog cannot close its mouth, use your fingers to lever the foreign body out.

5. If you are unable to remove the foreign body, lift the dog, hold it upside down by the hind legs and shake the dog vigorously to dislodge the foreign body and clear the airway.

6. If the foreign body does not dislodge, apply forceful, sudden pressure to the abdomen at the edge of the breastbone (use a fist or knee, depending on the size of the dog).

7. If the dog is not breathing, give mouth to nose resuscitation.

8. Hold the dog's muzzle closed and place your mouth over the dog's nose.

9. Slowly blow air into the dog's nose so that its chest expands.

Transporting an Injured Dog

1. Create a stretcher by placing a towel, rug, blanket, or coat on the ground next to the injured dog.

2. Take the dog by the scruff of the neck in a firm grip and pull the dog onto the stretcher.

Choking

1. Wedge something, such as the handle of a screwdriver, between the molar teeth on one side of the dog's mouth to keep it open.

2. Inspect the back of the throat, roof of the mouth and between the teeth for a foreign body.

First Aid For Common Health Problems

Foxtails

Foxtails are seeds that look like wheat. It is critical that a foxtail be removed as soon as it is discovered. Foxtails can be inhaled through the nasal cavity; they can burrow into the ears or eyes, between the toes, and under the skin. They move through the body, forming abscesses and creating serious infection. The results are often serious and can, if untreated, be fatal. Symptoms to look for include:

▼ Pawing at the ears—shaking the head.

▼ Rubbing an eye or squinting.

▼ Rubbing the head on the ground and wheeling in circles or licking and biting at the rectum or other parts of the body.

▼ Repeated violent sneezing, sometimes with a bloody discharge from the nostrils.

▼ Yelping or whining for no obvious reason.

▼ A small raised infected spot showing signs of inflammation.

Clusters of these barbed seeds can penetrate the skin and cause deep wounds and abscesses. In most cases removal of a foxtail entails placing the dog under anesthesia. Foxtails are a medical emergency!

Ear Disease

Ear disease is one of the most frequently seen problems in a small animal veterinary practice. The primary causes of ear disease are: parasites such as ear mites; fungal and bacterial infections; allergies and skin disorders; trauma caused by foreign objects (foxtails) or a self-inflicted injury; or a disorder in the wax-secreting glands within the ear.

Question: Why do golden retrievers have problems with their ears?

Answer: The ear canal is a moist, dark environment with very little air circulation. Because of the ear's design, it provides the perfect environment for bacterial and yeast infections to grow. The well-furred earflaps that lay down over golden retrievers' ears, predispose them to ear infections.

Question: What are the symptoms of ear disease?

Answer: You will notice your pet shaking its head or rubbing its ears against the carpet or outdoors in the grass. Your dog may also scratch excessively, and you may notice thick, red, inflamed skin on the outer ear. An infection of the outer or inner ear can be painful and frequently produces a foul-smelling, thick, waxy, yellow/black discharge. If it is not treated, the infection advances to the canals of the middle ear, and your dog may tilt his or her head or loose his or her balance and coordination. This is a very serious infection, sometimes requiring surgical drainage of the ear. Check your golden's ears on a weekly basis, more if the dog is in water on a regular basis. Normal ears are free of any odor and have a slight pinkish-white color. The skin is soft and elastic, not hard, thickened, or crusty. Do not try to diagnose an ear problem yourself. It is important that your veterinarian identifies the primary cause and determines the proper treatment. For instance, an ear mite infection requires one treatment, while a yeast or bacterial infection requires another protocol, and a skin allergy involves yet another course of treatment.

How To Clean Your Dog's Ears

1. Read label directions on bottle of ear cleaner; some require rinsing with warm water after cleaning.

2. Hold your dog's head still and with the earflap laid back, squeeze the bottle containing a wax dissolving solution so it completely fills the external ear canal. DO NOT force solution into the canal under pressure.

3. Place a clean, dry cotton ball at the entrance to the ear canal and gently massage the base of the ear working the solution from deep in the canal to the outer surface.

Replace the cotton ball periodically to absorb the solution and wax debris. Repeat if necessary until all the debris has been removed.

Hot Spots (Acute Moist Dermatitis)

Hot spots are common in golden retrievers. The combination of a double coat, water, heat, a fleabite, or flea allergy all contribute to the breed's propensity to develop this condition. As a golden retriever owner, it is important that you understand this condition and have on hand the various products to treat the hot spot as soon as you notice it.

Daily grooming and checking your dog for skin lesions such as a hot spot are an important part of caring for the health and well-being of your dog.

The problem is much more common in hot humid weather and may have something to do with lack of ventilation in the coat. A typical lesion is red, moist, and oozing. There is a crust in the center of the area surrounded by a halo of red skin. The hair is lost from the area, but the margins are sharply defined from the surrounding normal skin and hair. The lesion progresses rapidly if appropriate therapy is not started at once. Hot spots are often located near infected ears, anal sacs, and fleabites on the rump.

Hot spots are caused by a dog biting, rubbing, or scratching at a part of its body in an attempt to relieve an itch or pain. The itching creates an "itch-scratch" cycle. This cycle can produce several large sores within a few hours!

Often the scratching, biting, etc., are in response to a fleabite hypersensitivity, allergic skin disorder, inflammation of the ear, foreign body in the coat, dirty coat, or other painful muscular or skeletal disorder.

The author suggests keeping on hand several products to use at the first sign of a hot spot. If it does not respond within twenty-four hours or has spread, CONSULT YOUR VETERINARIAN.

Remedy 1

Trim or clip the surrounding hair (a real "bummer" if you are showing your dog). Apply Gold Bond Powder—check every couple of hours and reapply. This takes the itch/pain away and generally stops the dog from scratching. If you need to, put a protective plastic collar/bonnet on the dog to keep it from chewing the area, or protect the head area from scratching. Collars are available from your veterinarian.

Remedy 2

Clip off the hair, clean the area with hydrogen peroxide 3% mixed with a little water. Apply a spray such as Terra Cortril, Gentocin, Allercaine, etc. All are available from your veterinarian, pet supply store, or a catalog.

For severe hot spots, cortisone is recommended to remove the severe itching. This is available from your veterinarian and can quickly help break the itch-scratch cycle.

Keeping your golden brushed, clean, and flea free will aid in preventing hot spots.

Chapter 10
Grooming Your Golden Retriever

A hh! A subject dear to my heart; I love to groom my dogs. It is our quiet time together. It beats ironing, and the results are so rewarding. I guarantee you that if you follow the instructions in this chapter, both you and your dog will be happier.

- ▼ Grooming Products and Supplies
- ▼ What is Grooming?
- ▼ Getting Started
- ▼ Bathing and Drying
- ▼ Trimming Hair
- ▼ Grooming the Ears
- ▼ Trimming Nails

It's just mud!

Photo: Ginger Garrett

Grooming Products and Supplies

The products listed below are my favorites. You may find others that suit your taste or pocketbook. I consider the BASIC equipment to be the pin brush, comb, canine blow dryer, grooming table/grooming surface, and a hot/cold water supply for bathing.

Tools

- ▼ Pin Brush—#1 All Systems
- ▼ Natural Hair Bristle Brush—#1 All Systems
- ▼ Soft Slicker Brush—#1 All Systems
- ▼ Greyhound Comb—Metal Comb
- ▼ Flea Comb
- ▼ Dematting Rake
- ▼ Nail Grinding Tool or Nail Clippers
- ▼ Scissors and Thinning Shears
- ▼ Stripping Knives, (3) Various Size Blades
- ▼ Grooming Table—General Cage Model—Medium size
- ▼ Canine Blow Dryer—Challengaire 2000
- ▼ Tropic Shower—hot/cold water adaptor for washing machine faucet
- ▼ Booster Bath (a portable tub)

Shampoos And Conditioners

- ▼ #1 All Systems Super Cleaning and Conditioning shampoo

- ▼ #1 All Systems Rich Protein Lotion Conditioner

- ▼ #1 All Systems Self Rinse Shampoo
  (especially during winter months)

- ▼ #1 All Systems Coat Re-Texturizer and Skin Stabilizer

▼ #1 All Systems Tea Tree Oil Spray
(antibacterial, antifungal, antiseptic, analgesic)

▼ #1 All Systems Self Rinse Shampoo (a must in Winter)

Other Shampoos I like:

▼ Pure Pearl Shampoo and Conditioner
▼ Bio Groom Shampoo
▼ Traleigh Shampoo and Conditioner

What Is Grooming?

Grooming is a very general term that encompasses the various steps that one takes to maintain a dog's coat, nails, ears, and teeth in top condition. If grooming is done on a regular basis—daily or weekly—the job is easier for the dog and the groomer. If you neglect to groom your golden, you will pay the price—BIG dollars for professional grooming to remove mats, tangles, etc. There are numerous benefits derived when you groom your golden on a regular basis. Your dog will feel good, he'll be easier to groom—no mats, tangles, dirt, or fleas—and your home will be much easier to clean, so you'll welcome him inside more often. Plus, he'll look good! If you are grooming your puppy or have an older dog who is uneasy about being groomed, start slowly and work in increments. Daily brushing of the dog's coat and weekly nail trims are the way to begin.

How Often Should I Bathe My Dog?

Bathe as frequently as needed. How frequently will depend on your lifestyle and the dog's environment. Is your dog swimming or running through brush and mud? Are fleas a problem? Does he smell? If so, you'll want to bathe him. If you own a canine blow dryer, you will have to bathe less often because the dead hair and dirt come off each time you groom him.

How Long Does It Take to Groom a Golden?

Let me answer this question by spelling out my grooming routine.

Daily Sessions

I groom every day. Each session consists of lightly misting the coat with a spray bottle filled with a tablespoon of *conditioner* mixed with water. Then I use the *canine blow dryer* to blow out the excess hair and dirt. I brush the dog while I blow the hair—thereby removing tangles and mats. I check ears, eyes, and feet and remove any tangles or foreign matter lodged in the coat. This daily grooming takes me between five and ten minutes.

Weekly Grooming

Dogs being shown and puppies in training are bathed and trimmed on a weekly basis. Other dogs are bathed every ten days to two weeks during the summer and about every three weeks during the winter. Since my dogs all come in the house on a daily basis, the frequent bathing and daily brush/blowing out of the coat helps keep the house clean and also eliminates that "doggy" odor. The time it takes to bathe and blow dry a golden depends on the size of the dog and the amount of hair coat she has. A small puppy with less coat will take considerably less time than an adult in full coat. Bathing and drying a dog that is up to nine months of age should take about forty-five minutes. Bathing and drying an adult golden with a full coat can take an hour and a half.

One way to speed up the process is to bathe the dog, towel dry it, and place it in the crate. If you are using a Double K—Challengaire Dryer, they come with a small attachment that you can put on the end of the hose. This attachment clips onto the front of a crate. Turn on the dryer and let the air circulate around the dog while it is in the crate. Be sure to check the dog and don't leave her in the crate longer than it takes to get her seventy-five percent dry. Leave her a little water, so if she is thirsty, she can drink. If you're using a wire crate, you will need to cover it with a sheet or towels so the air doesn't escape. Remove her from the crate, let her out to "potty" (don't let her roll in the dirt), put her back on the grooming table, and finish drying her so that her coat is smooth and lays properly.

Getting Started

What Is a Grooming Table?

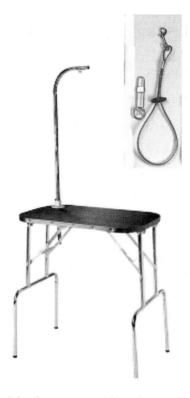

A grooming table is a specially constructed table that comes in various sizes and heights to fit different breeds of dogs. They range from very small (ringside tables), used for small breeds, to large fancy ones with hydraulic lifts, used by professional groomers and veterinarians. The table I recommend is moderately priced and will suit a golden retriever just fine. I do recommend that you invest in the grooming table and use it. Once your dog is used to it, grooming him will be easier for both of you. If you don't want to purchase a table, you can use any table that is waist height, such as a barbeque table. If you do, make sure that it is very stable and that you place a *non-skid* mat or topping on the table.

Getting Your Dog Accustomed to the Table

It is easier if you are working with a puppy because it is smaller, however, the same principles apply to an older dog. FIRST and foremost, we want the experience to be pleasant and routine. If you are working with a puppy:

1. Begin by placing him on the table and holding him with both hands so that he can't jump off. Talk to him softly and offer him a treat. Don't try to brush him yet, just talk to him and place him in a standing position. You just want to get him used to the feel of the table under his feet. If he wiggles or fights you, pick him up with one had under his jaw and the other between his hind legs and rock him back and forth *with his feet off the table*. Then set him down. He'll quickly figure out that having his feet on the table is a

better alternative than being rocked in the air. Continue to place him on the table and ask him to stand while you stroke him and talk to him—several times a day for two days.

2.   When he is comfortable on the table, the next step is to begin by brushing him with a soft brush. Continue to hold him with one hand so he won't jump off. Don't attempt to brush him *until* he remains quietly on the table. Don't baby him. If he is still wiggling and trying to get away, you haven't been firm enough—continue rocking and helping him figure out that his feet on the table is a GOOD THING. Brush gently and quickly for just a short time. Praise your puppy and give him a treat. Again, put him on the table for very short periods of time several times a day.

3.   When he is comfortable with the brush, begin with the blow dryer. Set it on low and quickly blow him all over. I find that most puppies try to bite the nozzle and play with it. To begin with, I let them—I make a game of it, but I also make sure I blow all over their body. Then I turn it off, give a quick brush, treats, a hug, and off they go. Within a couple of weeks, your puppy should be very comfortable and remain quiet while you brush him. If you are having trouble with the blower, have someone help hold the puppy. I don't use a grooming noose because I don't want to frighten him, nor do I want anything to interfere with him learning to relax and stay on the table. My goal is for the puppy to learn to accept the whole grooming process as part of his daily routine.

Hint: If you put your dog on the grooming table before you take him in the house, he'll learn to associate the table with entry to the house. My dogs run to the grooming table and jump on, because they know grooming leads to house time!

Getting the Older Dog Used to a Grooming Table

It is best to begin this process using two people. An adult golden is strong, and it is easier on all concerned if both of you lift him onto the table. Begin by placing his front paws on the table. One person should hold his paws in place and talk to him while the other lifts his hind legs up and onto the table. The adult dog will probably respond in one of two ways: 1) he'll freeze in place on his belly; or 2) he'll try to jump right off.

If He Freezes

Simply talk to him quietly and begin to brush him. Offer him a treat (he may refuse because he's too nervous). Just go about your business brushing and talking like it's the natural thing to do. When you feel him begin to relax, tell him, "good boy," and encourage him to jump off the table. If the dog is not a fully mature adult—DO NOT let him jump off—lift him off.

If He Tries to Jump Off the Table

Make an effort to keep him from jumping off. If he does jump off, go to him, bring him back to the table, and start over again. You may have to do this several times. Whatever you do—DON'T give up and let him get away with jumping off. He will have learned that he can get away with that behavior. Keep this up several times a day. When he begins to relax, try giving him a treat. If he takes the treat, begin to brush. When he accepts the brush, try feeding him on the table. I often feed an older dog on the table. Give them both meals on the grooming table, and you will find they'll jump on it to eat and begin to relax. Again, if you take the dog into the house immediately following the grooming table routine, he will begin to think it is a "good thing." Let's assume that he is now on the table and you have to restrain him from jumping off. That's OK. Talk to him quietly, get him to the point where he begins to relax, then lift him off, or give him a RELEASE COMMAND— "OK" and let him jump off. Again, if it is not a mature adult dog, don't let him jump and injure himself—lift him off.

Bathing and Trimming

These instructions assume you have the BASIC equipment—a grooming table, brushes, comb, blow dryer, scissors, and thinning shears. If you don't, you have something to work toward. If trimming the excess hair is not your "cup of tea," you might begin with the bathing, brushing, and drying and take your dog to a professional groomer for the trimming. It's easier for both you and your dog if you bathe and trim him in two sessions. You'll want to bathe first and be sure the dog is dry before you begin trimming the excess hair. Trimming a dirty dog will ruin a good pair of scissors. Be particularly careful when grooming your puppy to break up the session so the puppy doesn't get tired.

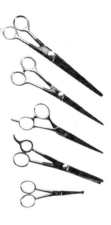

To Begin

1. Set up the grooming table outside or use your BOOSTER BATH and turn on your TROPIC SHOWER. (See Appendix.) If this is not an option, use your bathtub or shower stall with a hose and spray nozzle adapter. Both of the latter options are messier and less comfortable for both you and the dog. Dogs prefer to be bathed in warm water—not hot, not cold, but warm. The water temperature for a baby's bath will suit a golden just perfectly.

2. Brush out your dog's coat, and remove any tangles or foreign matter. You may also place cotton in his ears and a drop of mineral oil in his eyes.

3. Wet down your dog with warm water, beginning at the neck (not the head). After you have rinsed the dog's body, move to the head, being careful to avoid the eyes and inside of the ears. To close the ear, gently squeeze the base of the ear with one hand while rinsing with the other.

4. Apply the shampoo, beginning at the neck and working back toward the tail. Be sure to apply shampoo to the legs, under the belly, and under the buttocks. Next, work the shampoo up around the dog's head and ears, avoiding the actual eye area. The reason you begin at the neck is so the dog won't shake. Dogs shake water or other fluids off when their heads become wet. Most "dog" shampoos are supposed to be diluted. Read the directions on the bottle. I keep a special plastic bottle with a squeeze tip just for my shampoo mixture. You can also use a measuring cup or plastic pitcher. Be sure to dilute according to directions.

5. Work the shampoo into a lather, and gently massage your dog's entire body. To give him a lovely massage, work your fingers gently down his backbone and down to the end of his tail, pulling just a bit on the tail. You can actually feel your dog relax.

6. Rinse thoroughly and apply any conditioner according to manufacturer directions. After you have applied the conditioner, rinse thoroughly. If you have a conditioner that is to be left in the coat, be sure to rinse the dog very thoroughly before applying the conditioner. I generally rinse until I believe all the soap is out and then give the dog one more rinse just for good measure.

7. Towel dry the dog, beginning at his head and working toward the back. Dry the legs and feet thoroughly, then take him off the table on a leash and let him shake himself several times. If you are bathing in the bathroom, you might want to take him into the laundry room or garage to shake, hence the reason for the leash.

    It's now time to dry your dog. Don't tell me you didn't get the canine blow dryer—you'll be sorry!

8. After the shampoo has been applied, it is time to clean your dog's anal glands. The anal glands are located in small sacs just under the dog's rectum. Step to one side (so you don't get sprayed with very smelly anal fluid), gently squeeze the anal area between your thumb and forefinger. If there is excess fluid built up, it will come squirting out.

Keep squeezing until no more fluid appears. It is important to express the glands, as they can become infected and painful. If you see your dog "scooting" on his behind, he may be trying to find relief from anal glands that are full of excess fluid.

How to Use the Canine Blow Dryer

The key to successfully blow-drying a golden's coat is to blow-dry ninety-five percent of the dog's coat with the nozzle held *fairly close* to the dog's skin and blowing the hair in the *opposite* direction of the hair growth. Follow this by smoothing down the hair—blowing in the *same* direction the coat grows.

Challengaire 2000 Dryer
Courtesy of PetEdge

1. Blow against the coat all over the body, getting all the excess water off until seventy-five percent dry.

2. Blow with the coat to help the hair to lie properly.

3. Repeat blowing against the coat to complete the drying process to ninety-five percent.

4. Finish blowing with the coat to set the final pattern so the hair lies as smoothly as possible.

Ready–Set–Go

Establish a pattern. The purpose of establishing a pattern is so that you can remember where you are and what is already dry. You may establish any pattern you want. This is how I dry my dogs.

Drying the Body

Back: Holding the nozzle about one to two inches from the dog's body, with the end directed *against the hair*, work in sections or rows. Begin at the center of the spine over the buttock and work from the dog's rear forward to the withers. By working in rows, you can see the hair dry to the skin and it helps you maintain the pattern. **Note:** Because the dog can't see what you are doing and the dryer is noisy, he may become apprehensive. I find that gently holding an ear closed while working on the back and upper side makes for a happier dog, i.e., right side of back, hold right ear.

Sides: Dry along the back from the center of the spine, and move down one side from center spine to the middle of the rib cage. When you are at mid-rib cage, move the nozzle under the belly, and dry the underside of the dog working back up to the area along the rib cage that is already dry. Repeat this procedure on the other side of the dog.

Belly: Working from back to front, thoroughly dry belly hair pointing dryer nozzle up directly under the belly. Lift each front leg and dry under elbows and underside of chest. Continue up into the chest area, moving dryer nozzle further away from the dog and holding the ear on the side you are drying. If the dog is sensitive, turn dryer to lowest setting at this point.

Drying the Rear End

Facing the dog's buttocks, hold the nozzle approximately twelve inches away. This allows the hair on the back of the legs and buttocks to spread and dry all the way to the skin. While holding the nozzle in one hand, use your pin brush to gently brush through the hair as it dries. This procedure will remove any snarls or areas where the hair is "clumping" together. Dry the back legs and furnishings, including the tail. Dry the tail underneath and on top. When drying the top of the tail, hold the nozzle in the direction the hair grows. Make sure tail is totally dry. Putting dogs away with a wet tail can cause a "cold tail," which is painful, and it may be several days before the tail returns to *normal.*

Drying the Front Legs

Dry the front legs holding the nozzle close to the hair, pointing up against the natural growth of the hair. You may use a slicker brush (on the front of the leg only) to aid in drying. Some dogs and puppies are sensitive to the brush in this area; if so, go slowly and use the brush sparingly. You can achieve the desired result by pointing the nozzle of the dryer in the upward position. For the long hair (feathering) at the back of the front legs, hold the nozzle in the center so the hair spreads; use pin brush to remove tangles.

Drying the Head

Turn your dryer to the lowest setting. Be very cautious about allowing the forced air to go in the ear. I always hold an ear closed and often stroke the ear I'm holding as I dry the dog's head. If a young, inexperienced dog or puppy is not entirely comfortable with the drying process, I leave the head slightly damp. In other words, don't make a big deal of getting the head dry. It's more important to let a dog become adjusted to the whole process before attempting to get it perfect.

A Finished Look

Blow the hair in the direction it grows. Hold the nozzle approximately six inches from the dog. Begin at the top of the head, and work back to the tail drying and brushing the coat with a natural bristle brush or pin brush in the direction the hair grows. At this point, you are smoothing the hair down and taking out as much curl (if any) as possible. Complete the job by thoroughly combing through the dog's coat with a greyhound comb. *Voila!* A beautifully groomed golden retriever.

Tag at 9 months of age—
a beautifully groomed puppy.

Photo: Jerry Vavra

Trimming Hair

Trimming Feet

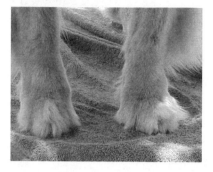

The photos in this section are courtesy of the author.

Photos by: Sylvia Donahey-Feeney

1. Use your small six-and-one-half-inch straight scissors. Begin by trimming away the excess hair on the bottom of the foot and between the pads. Do not trim the hair between the toes; this will be trimmed later using thinning shears.

2. Next, trim around the outside edge of the foot following the natural line of the foot. This is the area alongside of each toenail where the hair on the foot meets the side of the black pad.

3. Take your small slicker brush or a soft brush and brush the hair on the foot up, opposite the direction in which it grows. As you do this, you will see long tufts of hair coming out from between the dog's toes.

4. Use your thinning shears. Hold the thinning shears with the point angled up and a little sideways; trim the tufts.

5. Brush them back down, and you should have a neat foot with a light covering of hair over the top. You don't want to trim it so close that you can see all the spaces between the toes.

6. Use six-and-one-half-inch scissors. After brushing the hair down, make final adjustments to the perfect cat's foot by using your straight scissors to give a final finished look to the outside edges of the foot and toes.

Trimming Hock Hair

1. Dampen hair on hocks and comb hair out away from leg. If hock hair is extremely long, cut it to mid-length with six-and- one-half-inch scissors. Comb again so that hair stands out away from leg and you have a straight line of hair to cut.

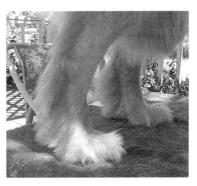

2. Use six-and-one-half-inch scissors, and trim hair to about one and one-half to two inches. Begin cutting from top to bottom in a clean straight line. When the hair is the correct length, brush (small slicker brush or comb) the hair straight up, beginning at the bottom of the hock.

3. Use thinning shears. Round off hard edges of the hair with the thinning shears, brushing and combing up until hock hair is contoured and neat.

Grooming Ears

An ungroomed dog head and ears

1. Begin by trimming all the excess hair from around the outside bottom and outside edges of the dog's ear. Use your thinning shears. Trim the outside edge of the ear. Begin at the bottom (longest point) of the ear and trim along the outside edge, moving the shear toward the back of the dog's head. Go back to the longest point and square off the bottom of the ear. To square off, simply trim the tip or end of the ear in a straight line. Then, gently round the edges of the straight line. This allows you to follow the contour of the ear and presents a soft appearance. Now trim the short area between the bottom of the ear and the flap. Begin just above the bottom of the ear (the portion you have just worked on). Pointing the tip of the shear up, follow the edge of the ear up to the bottom of the flap.

2. To groom the ear flap (outside of the entire ear), brush the hair on the outside of the ear up, opposite the direction in which it grows. Using your thinning shears, begin about one inch below the top of the ear where it meets the head and in from the front flap, (that small piece at the very front of the ear that turns back). The thinning shears should be pointed up toward the top of the ear. Take small incremental snips moving from right to left across the ear. Brush the hair down and remove the cut hair. Start again just below where you left off, and repeat this process until you have reached the bottom of the ear. After every three or four snips, comb the hair down and look at the results. You should not see any scissor marks.

3. To trim the excess hair from the front flap, point the tip of the thinning shears DOWN. This is the only time the tip will be pointed down when trimming ears. This allows you to trim with the grain of the hair. Snip the hair once or twice and brush out. When it is neat, stop trimming.

Trimming Your Dog's Nails

Clipping your dog's nails can be a challenge. You will probably feel like Hulk Hogan, wrestling your puppy in order to handle her flailing paws. Trust me, with the right amount of gentle restraint and a firm voice, you can master the art of trimming nails. Once mastered, it will serve you in good stead for the life of your dog.

If, at first, your puppy is resistant (up to three months of age), it helps to have someone else hold her while you trim. The goal is to make trimming a routine, nonthreatening experience. Take your time, and speak softly to the puppy.

Most people fear trimming nails because they don't want to hurt the dog. Trimming a dog's nails is just like trimming your own. It doesn't hurt unless you get too close. A dog usually protests more from having its foot and toes held than from the actual trimming itself.

As puppies become older, they also wiggle and protest a bit more. If you are persistent and trim weekly, they soon become used to it and sit or stand quietly.

How to Trim Nails

Begin the nail trimming process using two people. One holds the puppy and the other gently takes her paw and clips the very end of each nail using a regular human fingernail clipper. If she struggles, be gentle but persistent. Do this with a young (seven-to-nine-week) old puppy a couple of times  a week. That way you only take off a very small portion of the nail, and she gets used to the process.

You can see the light tip of new nail growth at the end of your puppy's nail; just clip off that portion. If you hit the quick, it is painful for a brief moment. Your puppy will remember this and become more resistant. If you do hit the quick, just wet your finger, stick it into the Kwik-Stop powder, and dab it on the end of the nail. This will stop the bleeding.

Remember how, as a child, you used to hold your fingers over a flashlight and "see through your fingers"? You can use this same technique on your puppy, but with a penlight flashlight. Hold the beam directly under the nail, and you will see the quick. It may be easier to lay the penlight on the surface of your grooming table, or whatever surface the puppy is lying on, to eliminate the need for a third hand. Sometimes black nails are too dense for light rays to penetrate, and it is harder to see the quick. This method works especially well for that type of nail. In any case, make smaller clips until you reach the gristle-like area just before the quick.

I switch to the large toenail clippers when the puppy is about nine weeks, and by the time they are three months old, they are ready for the standard dog nail clipper or nail grinder.

Tools of the Trade

I prefer the nail grinder. Although it is "noisier," the results are better and you are less likely to hit the quick. The noise may startle the puppy, but if you begin early enough—around ten weeks—you will be amazed at how calm the dog will become. It is a matter of conditioning (repeating the process over and over on a regular basis) that helps create a stress-free grooming session when it comes time to do the nails. My four-month-old puppy lies quietly on my bed while I grind her toes and happily takes her "good girl" treat when we are finished.

If you want to continue to use a nail clipper, purchase a high quality clipper with an adjustable piece between the blades. This allows you to adjust for the amount of nail you want to trim back and is added protection against taking too much nail off and cutting the dog's quick.

Chapter 11

The Versatile Golden Retriever

The golden retriever's adaptability and pleasant disposition allow him to perform a variety of tasks and functions. This versatility is a hallmark of the breed. To provide you with up-to-date information on performance activities such as field training, hunting, agility, tracking, obedience, and search and rescue, I asked the experts for help. With the exception of the section on conformation events, which was written by the author, all of the sections in this chapter were written by people whom I consider to be experienced, reputable, and highly regarded. A brief biography of the contributing author appears before each of the sections. Some of the contributing authors have books or videos available. Their products are listed in the Appendix section.

▼ Conformation   Maryle Malloy
▼ Agility   Chris Miele
▼ Tracking   Ed and Marallyn Wight
▼ Obedience   Connie Cleveland
▼ Field   Jackie Mertens
▼ Hunting   Doug and Judy Spink
▼ Search and Rescue   Kathryn L. Jones

Dog Shows–Conformation Events

Dog shows (conformation events) are intended to evaluate breeding stock. The size of these events ranges from large all-breed shows, with more than three thousand dogs entered, to small local specialty club shows, featuring a specific breed. The dog's conformation (overall appearance and structure), an indication of the dog's ability to produce quality puppies, is judged.

Types of Conformation Dog Shows

There are three types of conformation dog shows.

▼ **All-breed shows** offer competitions for more than 150 breeds and varieties of dogs recognized by the AKC. All-breed shows are the type often shown on television.

▼ **Specialty shows** are restricted to dogs of a specific breed or to varieties of one breed. For example, the Golden Retriever Club of America's show is for golden retrievers only, but the Poodle Club of America's specialty show includes the three varieties of the Poodle—Standard, Miniature, and Toy.

▼ **Group shows** are limited to dogs belonging to one of the seven groups. For example, the Potomac Hound Group show features only breeds belonging to the Hound group.

Which Dogs May Participate

To be eligible to compete, a dog must:

▼ Be individually registered with the American Kennel Club.

▼ Be six months of age or older.

▼ Be a breed for which classes are offered at a show.

▼ Meet any eligibility requirements in the written standard for its breed.

Spayed or neutered dogs are not eligible to compete in conformation classes at a dog show, because the purpose of a dog show is to evaluate breeding stock.

In the show ring—an outstanding example of a Golden Retriever bitch —Ch. Birnam Wood's Austintatious

The Role of the Judge

Judges examine the dogs, then give awards according to how closely each dog compares to the judge's mental image of the "perfect" dog described in the breed's **official standard**.

The standard describes the characteristics that allow the breed to perform the function for which it was bred. These standards include specifications for structure, temperament, and movement. The official written standard for each breed is maintained by the breed's national club and is included in *The Complete Dog Book* published by the AKC. The judges are experts on the breeds they judge. They examine ("go over") each dog with their hands to see if the teeth, muscles, bones, and coat texture conform to the breed's standard. They view each dog in profile for overall balance and watch each dog gait ("move") to see how all of those features fit together in action.

How a Dog Show Works

Each dog presented to a judge is exhibited ("handled") by its owner, breeder, or a hired professional. The role of a handler is similar to that of a jockey who rides a horse around the track and, hopefully, into the winner's circle.

The author handling Ch. Goodtimes Singing Inthe Rain to a Best of Opposite Sex win.

Photo: Rich Bergman

Most dogs in competition at conformation shows are competing for points toward their AKC championships. It takes fifteen points, including two majors (wins of three, four, or five points) awarded by at least three different judges, to become an American Kennel Club "Champion of Record."

The number of championship points awarded at a show depends on the number of males ("dogs") and females ("bitches") of the breed actually in competition. The larger the entry, the greater the number of points a male or a female can win. The maximum number of points awarded to a dog at any show is five points.

Males and females compete separately within their respective breeds, in six regular classes. Divided by sex, the following classes are offered:

Puppy   Dogs between six and twelve months of age that are not yet champions.

12-18 Months Dogs twelve to eighteen months of age that are not yet champions.

Novice   Dogs that have never won a blue ribbon in any of the other classes or have won fewer than three first-place ribbons in the Novice class.

Bred By Exhibitor   The dog is not yet a champion, and the exhibitor is the breeder and the owner.

American-Bred   A dog whose parents were mated in America, and who was born in America. The dog is not yet a champion.

Open   Any dog of the breed, at least six months of age. After these classes are judged, all the dogs that won first place in a class compete again to see who is the best of the winning dogs. Males and females are judged separately. Only the best male (Winners Dog) and the best female (Winners Bitch) receive championship points. The Winners Dog and Winners Bitch then compete with the champions for the Best of Breed award. At the end of the Best of Breed Competition, three awards are usually given.

Best of Breed   The dog judged as the best in its breed category.

Best of Winners   The dog judged as the better of the Winners Dog and Winners Bitch.

Best of Opposite Sex   The best dog that is the opposite sex to the Best of Breed winner.

The Road to Best in Show

Dog shows are a process of elimination, with one dog being named **Best in Show** at the end of the show. To compete for **Best in Show**, a dog must be a Group Winner.

Only the Best of Breed winners advance to compete in the **Group** competitions. Each AKC-recognized breed falls into one of seven group classifications. The seven groups are Sporting, Hound, Working, Terrier, Toy, Non-Sporting and Herding. Four placements are awarded in each group, but only the first-place winner advances to the Best in Show competition.

The Seven Groups in All-Breed Shows

Sporting
These dogs were bred to hunt game birds both on land and in the water. The breeds in this group include pointers, retrievers, setters, and spaniels.

Hounds
These breeds were bred for hunting other game by sight or scent. These breeds include such dogs as beagles, bassets, Dachshunds, and greyhounds.

Working
These dogs were bred to pull carts, guard property, and perform search and rescue services. Among the breeds in this group are the Akita, boxer, Doberman pinscher, and St. Bernard.

Terrier
This group includes breeds such as the Airedale terrier, cairn terrier, and Scottish terrier. Terriers were bred to rid property of vermin such as rats.

Toy
These dogs were bred to be household companions. This group includes little dogs such as the Chihuahua, Maltese, Pomeranian, and pug.

Non-Sporting
This diverse group includes the chow chow, bulldog, Dalmatian, and poodle. These dogs vary in size and function, and many are considered companion dogs.

Herding
These dogs were bred to help shepherds and ranchers herd their livestock. The briard, collie, German shepherd, and Old English sheepdog are some of the breeds in this group.

The seven group winners are brought into the ring where they compete for Best in Show, the highest award at a dog show. Only one dog is chosen from the Group Winners to receive this prestigious award; that dog is awarded Best in Show. On any given day, the dog that wins this award may have defeated up to three thousand dogs!

Carley Simpson and Trina, Ch. Quillmark's Spring Fling, CD, OD   Photo: Jerry Vavra

Ribbons

Each dog that receives an award is given a ribbon by the judge. The color of the ribbon indicates the type of award the dog has won.

Blue	Awarded for first place in any regular class. Also awarded to the winner of each group competition, usually in the form of a "rosette."
Red	Awarded for second place in each class. Also awarded for second place in each group competition, usually in the form of a "rosette."
Yellow	Awarded for third place in each class. Also awarded for third place in each group competition, usually in the form of a "rosette."
White	Awarded for fourth place in each class. Also awarded for fourth place of each group competition, usually in the form of a "rosette."
Purple	Awarded to the winners of the Winners Dog and Winners Bitch classes. Since these are the classes in which championship points are earned, these ribbons are highly coveted.

Purple and White	Awarded to the Reserve Winners, that is, the runners up to the winner of the Winners Dog and Winners Bitch classes.
Blue and White	Awarded to the dog that wins Best of Winners, that is, the better of the Winners Dog and Winners Bitch winners.
Purple and Gold	Awarded to the dog judged "Best of Breed" in each breed competition. This is highly coveted because it allows advancement to the Group competition.
Red and White	Awarded to the Best of Opposite Sex. This means the best dog of the breed that is the opposite sex of the Best of Breed winner.

Junior Showmanship

The AKC offers youngsters ten to eighteen years of age the opportunity to compete with others their own age at various AKC events. Juniors competing in conformation events are judged on how they present their dogs.

Nicki Madrigrano and Mini, Ch. Goodtimes Singing Inthe Rain. At the age of 11, Nicki handled Mini to a Best of Breed win at the prestigious Westminster Kennel Club show.

Dog Show Terms

Angulation Angles created by bones meeting at their joints.

Baiting Using liver or some treat to get the dog's attention and have him look alert.

Bench Show A dog show at which the dogs are kept on assigned benches when not being shown in competition, so they can be viewed and discussed by attendees, exhibitors, and breeders.

Exhibitor A person who brings a dog to a dog show and shows it in the appropriate class.

Fancier A person who is especially interested, and usually active, in some phase of the sport of purebred dogs.

Gait The way a dog moves; movement is a good indicator of structure and condition.

Groom To brush, comb, trim, or otherwise make a dog's coat neat.

Handler A person or agent who takes a dog into the show-ring or who works the dog at a field trial or other performance event.

Heel A command to a dog to keep close beside its handler.

Match Show A usually informal dog show at which no championship points are awarded.

Miscellaneous Class Transitional class for breeds attempting to advance to full AKC recognition.

Pedigree The written record of a dog's family tree of three or more generations.

Points Credits earned toward a championship.

Soundness Mental and physical well-being.

Stacking	Posing the dog's legs and body to create a pleasing picture. Additional terms can be found on the AKC web site www.akc.org.

Preparing Your Golden Retriever for the Showring

Your beautiful baby has arrived. You're already picturing a purple and gold rosette with your name on it! Hold that thought—but get to work preparing your dog for competition. You will need the right combination of feed, grooming, play training, and socialization before you're both ready. To help you, I'm going to share with you all the things I do to get my dog ready to compete in the breed ring.

The Right Diet

No matter how hard you work brushing, cleaning, and trimming your dog, if you are not feeding a high quality food, the coat will tell the story. Creating a winning look is a combination of proper feed, exercise/conditioning, grooming, and training. That being said, here's what I recommend. I feed my golden puppies Eukanuba Large Breed puppy food. Follow the recommendation of your breeder, but do feed a product that is made especially for large breeds that grow rapidly. Feeding a food too high in protein and fat can push growth too fast and create problems in the joints, ligaments, and bones of a rapidly growing puppy.

Rule # 1–Stack Every Day

What Is a "Stack"?

Stacking is the term for placing a dog in a particular stance or standing position. This position may be held for an indefinite period of time while the dog is being exhibited and/or examined by the judge. Different breeds are often "stacked" in a manner specific to that breed.

Preparing for the show ring—Sax, Goodtimes Little Boy Blue pictured at 10 weeks of age with his new owner, Pablo Esteves.   Photo: Co-owner, Naiana Chierici

How to Teach Your Puppy to Stack

Before we teach puppies to stack, we teach them to stand, that is, stand still on the grooming table. Teaching a puppy to stack is a sequence of events. I start my puppies on the grooming table at five weeks of age, and by the time they are ready to go home, they stack quite nicely. For purposes of these instructions, let's assume that your puppy is eight to ten weeks old as you begin training. If the puppy is older or if you are working with an adult, you certainly won't be able to lift him and rock him to get him steady.

First I make sure the puppy is going to be comfortable. Placing a sheepskin pad or towel on the grooming table works well. I begin by kissing her, talking softly to her, and encouraging her to eat a small bite of kibble or cheese. When she is moderately comfortable, I place her feet squarely under her and ask her to stand for just a moment or two. I tease her with a cookie or piece of cheese and tell her she's "perfect." Then I give her the cheese and pick her up for a hug. If she's happy and comfortable, I may do this one or two more times during that session.

If your puppy doesn't want to stand or fusses around, pick her up with one hand gently placed behind the head and around the neck, and put the other hand between the hind legs. Pick the puppy up so her feet are off the table and rock her back and forth.

This will not hurt the puppy but has the effect of making her happy to have her feet on the table when you put her down. If necessary, continue the rocking procedure several times until she will stand quietly with all four feet on the table for a moment or two. Don't worry about the position of the feet; that comes later with practice.

Once your puppy is standing solidly on the table, you can begin to position the legs for a "stack." I continue to stack puppies on the grooming table until they are three and one-half to four months old, then I begin to stack them on the ground. They are more secure on the table when they are small, and it isn't so intimidating because they are much closer to your height. Consider how big we must seem to little puppies when they are on the ground and we are standing over them. I use the same pattern for stacking puppies on the table as I do when I begin to stack them on the ground. The only difference is that when I stack a baby puppy I don't use a collar. By the time the puppy is three months of age, you can use a soft cotton or nylon show collar.

The Stack Pattern

1. Make sure your collar is the right size. A soft nylon #16 works well on a puppy three to four months old. If it's too big, he can back out of it, and you don't have enough control. If it's too small, you can't maneuver well enough, and it is uncomfortable.

2. Place the collar high up on the neck and snug with the jaw-bone. Pull the collar gently up behind the ears and exert light pressure to raise the head. I stroke under the chin with my fingers to help relax the puppy.

3. Place his feet, and don't worry about anything else for a few days. When he is comfortable with where you have placed his feet and will stand still, run your hands over his back and other places on his body while you tell him to stand/stay.

4. When he will stand/stay solidly, the next step is to put pressure on his back by gently pushing down in several places. In addition, gently try to rock him from side to side.

When he remains steady, you are now ready to ask for the dog to perfect the stack position and hold it. Facing the dog's right side, set the collar in place high under the throat, behind the ears, and then position the legs. This is the sequence I generally use.

- Holding collar in right hand, gently bring it up so it sits behind ears and underneath where the throat meets the jaw line.

- Place left front leg (use left hand)

- Place right front leg (you will have switched collar to left hand)

- Place left rear (using right hand on collar and left on leg)

- Place right rear (using right hand on collar and left on leg)

- Position head based on judge's position

- Switch collar to left hand, bait right hand.

Note: Some dogs indicate a preference in training to have hind feet placed first, some move a foot consistently. Follow the order that suits your dog. There is no right way. The best way is the way that allows your dog to "put his best foot forward."

Baiting

Use your bait to encourage the dog to put its nose where you want it. For instance, put bait on the ground in front of the dog to encourage it to look at the bait but still hold the stack position. Use the bait to change the dog's eye and head position. When the judge is at a distance, looking at the profile of the dog, you want the dog to be rocked forward, looking a bit down. When the judge is in front of you, looking at the head and expression, you want the bait up and in front of the dog at eye level. This allows the judge to see the expression and keeps those ears up and forward, presenting the most pleasing appearance.

Mirrors

Use a mirror to perfect the stack. You can see exactly how far back the hind feet should be placed, how to position the front feet for the best appearance, and how your dog looks with various head positions.

Rule #2 – Groom Every Day

The Grooming Table

From the time you acquire your puppy, you should be grooming and playing with it on the grooming table. Keep the sessions short, and when you are through, take your puppy into the house. My dogs think that grooming is the best part of the day because they always come in the house when I've finished grooming. Even if you don't plan to do anything, put the puppy on the table, run a brush over him, stack him, give him a treat, and whisk him off to the house. If you follow this advice, your dog will be jumping on the grooming table as soon as it is big enough. Mine usually start trying by four months of age.

I never use a grooming noose on a young puppy. I work quietly brushing him and trimming feet and ears—a little at a time, several times a week. I don't care if he stands at this point; the goal is for him to accept what I am doing and to know it doesn't hurt. If your puppy is unusually busy or afraid, have someone hold the puppy while you trim the hair on the feet and ears. Use a small nail clipper on toenails, and do it every week. When grooming, go slowly and quietly. Don't ask too much too soon. If your puppy has been quiet and you sense him becoming uneasy, simply quit. Always finish by stacking and giving a treat. After my puppy remains calm and accepts grooming, I teach him to stand with the grooming noose on. Make sure your puppy is steady; it can be pretty traumatic to have a puppy thrash around and try to jump off the table with a noose on its neck. Oh yeah, I did learn this one the hard way.

Daily Grooming Routine

▼ Mist with conditioner
▼ Blow out coat
▼ Comb through

Weekly Grooming Routine

▼ Bathe
▼ Clean Ears
▼ Brush Teeth
▼ Trim Toenails

Bi-Weekly Grooming Routine

▼ Follow weekly routine, plus
▼ Trim feet
▼ Trim ears

Grooming Supplies and Tools You Need

▼ Challengaire 2000 Dryer
▼ Medium size grooming table, arm, and noose
▼ #1 All Systems—for Brushes and Shampoos
▼ Pin Brush—Large
▼ Slicker Brush—Medium
▼ Greyhound Comb
▼ Conditioning Shampoo
▼ Conditioner
▼ Self-Rinse Shampoo

See Chapter 9, "Grooming Your Golden Retriever," for more information.

Rule #3–Play, Train, and Socialize Every Day

At Home

I do things a little differently with a puppy I'm going to show at a rather early age than I might do if I were training a family pet or puppy for other performance events. I don't put a collar on the puppy until it is about three months old. Because my property and facilities are completely dog proof and safe, I can control my puppy safely.

My puppy helps me with "chores"—feeding, cleaning, and leaf blowing. I want him used to anything that is a part of our normal day. Most of the time, I don't use a collar. If I have to grab him for a correction, I grab him by the nape of the neck, as his mother would do. Isn't that what the loose skin on the neck is for? We go for walks in the yard and in our five-acre pasture. If you have the area and can do this, your puppy will really learn to follow you wherever you go. I keep "cookies" in my pocket, and when he gets interested in something, I practice a "recall." If he doesn't respond, I yell "cookie" and run the other way. It works most every time. If it doesn't, I go to him, grab him, and remind him I called. I want him to get used to going where I want and being with me without restraint. We're buddies.

If you don't have the luxury of lots of space, use your collar and leash. A word of warning though—don't leave a collar on your show puppy; it will quickly leave a rather permanent line around the neck.

Hit the Road, Jack!

Begin right away taking your puppy for short trips in the car. Go to the bank, the post office, get an ice cream (the best ride of all), take her to a quiet corner of a parking lot away from scary traffic. If you take her for a walk outside your favorite grocery store, she'll be ooh'd and aah'd by friendly children and adults. Take her someplace safe at least once a week and more often if possible. When she has had at least three vaccinations, you can take her to a puppy socialization class, but *no-no* to sits!

Teaching Your Dog to Gait (Move on the Lead)

I'm not going to attempt to teach movement in this chapter. It is critical that you participate in a handling class, seek the advice of a professional handler, or work with an experienced competitor to gain this knowledge. I will tell you this, correct movement—on the lead—is critical to success in the showring. Golden retrievers are a sporting breed, thus they are judged on movement. The prettiest outline in the world won't win in the breed ring unless that same dog can move in a smooth and fluid manner.

Ideally you should look for a conformation handling class, preferably one that has classes for different ages or sizes. Begin slowly. Just visit and let your puppy watch. Hold him and get him familiar with the surroundings. Never make your puppy go through a full session (forty-five to sixty minutes). I generally take a couple of dogs, work with the puppy for a short time, then move on to the next dog. Work up to longer sessions, but always quit before your puppy gets tired. If you can't find a conformation handling class in your area, get together with several friends. Look for fun matches and practice at the match. The best place to get information on handling classes in your area is through the local all-breed dog clubs. Don't have classes available? Start one. Get the people in your local golden retriever club to put together a weekly class.

Are You Ready for Your First Dog Show?

Before you enter your first show, you need to be ready.

Equipment

▼ Soft, fine leather lead
▼ Nylon collar, 16 to 18 inches
▼ New outfit for you!
▼ Table
▼ Dryer
▼ Electric cords, tack box, generator
▼ Exercise pen and mat

Training

Your dog is ready when he is:

▼ Crate trained—doesn't bark, sleeps quietly, and is able to wait in crate while you go about your business.

▼ He must be used to travel in the car.

▼ He must be socially adept with other dogs and people.

▼ He must hold a stack and bait.

▼ He must be able to move on leash: go down and back at proper speed, follow various patterns such as triangles, and return to the judge and stand square.

If you have the opportunity, work with another person's experienced show dog. An experienced dog "knows the ropes" and will give you the feeling of what it is like to handle a well-trained show dog.

If you are new to the sport, you will be nervous when you begin showing your puppy. It took two years before my butterflies left. Now I only get them when I watch someone else show my dogs.

At the Dog Show

Don't wear your puppy out by showing too much. Begin slowly, and choose venues that are pleasant. Make sure the weather is not too extreme—too hot or too cold. For instance, choose a three-day weekend of shows held outdoors in the spring. Not too hot, not too cold, no rain. Enter the second and third day only. On day one, let him experience the show site, dogs, commotion, and excitement of the show. Show him on day two, and if he is not too stressed and is having fun, show him the next day.

Give him lots of crate rest, and don't run him all over the place or keep him up all night. Let him stay in his crate or exercise pen and observe the action. This will give him something to think about. If he is stressed, just let him hang out the second day and don't show him. Please don't "over show" your puppy! I recommend that you only show young puppies one weekend per month. If you are showing an older dog, take the young one with you so it can hang out and play. As the dog gets older and is enjoying the experience, the time is right to increase the number of times you show.

It is not uncommon for an owner with a really nice puppy to burn the puppy out by showing too often. Dog shows are stressful. It's our job to make sure they are fun for everyone—especially the dog.

Unusual Behavior

I have observed puppies who are used to showing, suddenly become frightened and spooked. The first time this happened to me, it took me almost four months to get my puppy's head "screwed on straight." I took it slowly, hauled her everywhere, and made her start all over again. Too much pressure to begin with? Adolescence? Hormones? Maybe, but whatever the reason, I needed to rebuild her confidence. If this happens to you, try not to overact and blame yourself. Just go back to the basics and make life fun.

A BIG win—Barbara Madrigrano and Liz won the 6-9 month puppy class at the 1994 National Specialty show. At the tender age of 13 months, she earned her championship title. Liz —Ch. Goodimes Ruling Passion has produced numerous champions and Best In Show dogs and is a GRCA Outstanding dam.

Using a Professional Trainer

A final note. Many professional handlers have "puppy pro-
grams." They generally take puppies between the ages of five
months and twelve months in the puppy program. Sending puppies out for thirty days with a trusted handler can do wonders for
them. The handlers play with the puppies; the puppies get to
travel on the big truck with other dogs; they go to the dog show,
hang out, get walked around the show grounds, and learn to
relax and have fun. They will also be groomed daily, stacked, and
taught to gait on the lead. All in all, I have found this to be a great
investment. It's PUPPY CAMP.

Select your professional handler with care. Make sure he or
she shows goldens and loves them. Don't be afraid to talk with
several handlers. Observe them at ringside, visit their kennels, and
assure yourself that they will treat your puppy as well as or better
than you would. I know it is difficult to send a puppy away from
home, but the experience can be very rewarding. You're on the
mark, you're set, now go have fun, and bring home a ribbon or two.

Golden Retriever Club of America Titles

The GRCA awards titles in the following categories. The
requirements necessary to earn each title are shown on the web
site: grca.org. All of these titles are suffixes and appear after the
dog's registered name. For instance: Ch. Goodtimes Can't Stopthe
Rain, OS is an AKC champion of record, therefore the Ch. appears
before his name. He is a GRCA—Outstanding Sire, therefore the
OS appears after his name.

- ▼ Outstanding Sire
- ▼ Outstanding Dam
- ▼ Show Dog Hall of Fame
- ▼ Field Dog Hall of Fame
- ▼ Obedience Dog Hall of Fame
- ▼ Agility Dog Hall of Fame
- ▼ WC—Working Certificate (field/hunting)
- ▼ WCX—Working Certificate Excellent
- ▼ Versatility Certificate (Multiple events)
- ▼ Versatility Excellent Certificate

AKC Event Titles Applicable to Golden Retrievers

Prefix Title
AFC	Amateur Field Trial Champion
CH	Champion (Conformation)
CT	Champion Tracker (Tracking)
DC	Dual Champion (Conformation/Field)
FC	Field Trial Champion
NAFC	National Amateur Field Champion
NOC	National Obedience Champion
OTCH	Obedience Trial Champion:
TC	Triple Champion (Conformation/Field/Obedience)
MACH	Master Agility Champion
VCCH	Versatile Companion Champion

Suffix Title
AX	Agility Excellent
AXJ	Excellent Agility Jumper
CD	Companion Dog
CDX	Companion Dog Excellent
JH	Junior Hunter
MH	Master Hunter
MX	Master Agility Excellent
MXJ	Master Agility Jumper
NA	Novice Agility
NAJ	Novice Agility Jumper
OA	Open Agility
OAJ	Open Agility Jumper
SH	Senior Hunter
TD	Tracking Dog
TDX	Tracking Dog Excellent
UD	Utility Dog
UDX	Utility Dog Excellent
UDVST	Utility Dog Variable Surface Tracking
VCD1	Versatile Companion Dog 1
VCD2	Versatile Companion Dog 2
VCD3	Versatile Companion Dog 3
VCD4	Versatile Companion Dog 4
VST	Variable Surface Tracking

Agility

Chris Miele

Chris Miele is the regular agility columnist for the *Golden Retriever News* and a contributing writer for *Clean Run Magazine*. Chris has been an AKC agility judge since 1993 and has been invited to judge some of the most prestigious events including the Golden Retriever National Agility Trial and the American Kennel Club's National Agility Championships. Her students have earned several hundred titles in agility, including the very prestigious MACH title, and they include World Championship Gold Medal winners. Chris's own dogs each have agility titles including a MACH title for her youngest female, Piper. Chris has both breed and agility champion golden retrievers and has several dogs who have been ranked among the top ten in breed and in agility. She has owned goldens since 1982 under the kennel name of Cross Creek Goldens.

Dog agility, a new and exciting sport, began quietly as a game for the spectators at horse shows to entertain them during course changes. People soon started cheering for their favorite dogs as they went over the horse fences. This new sport went to the world famous Cruft's Dog Show in England as an exhibition in February 1978. It was an instant success. Just as the wonderful breed of golden retrievers came to America shortly after it was established in the United Kingdom, so did the sport of dog agility make its way to the United States in 1986. Today the sport has become one of the most popular events at dog shows, and there are agility training centers all across the country. Agility has been featured on many television shows and attracts all ages. At the competitions in the United States, you will see handlers from four years of age to more than eighty years of age all having a great time playing with their dogs.

So What Exactly Is Dog Agility?

Dog agility is a game consisting of an obstacle course designed by a judge where a team of dog and handler completes the course within a predetermined time. It is a sport where the dog, who has never seen that particular course, must navigate the

Casey's Golden Ace, CD, AX, AXJ, CGC, TDI pictured at 8 years of age.
Photo: Ken Gee

course of obstacles directed by a handler using hand signals, voice, and body language. There are increasing degrees of difficulty, depending on the level of competition, and there is a standard time set for the dogs to complete the course.

The Obstacle Course

Agility obstacles consist of several types: contact obstacles (dog walk, A-frame, and seesaw), tunnels (open or pipe tunnel and collapsed tunnel or chute), jumps and hurdles (tire jump, panel jump, spread jumps), plus weave poles and a table. The judge arranges these obstacles into sequences and challenges. Some obstacles may be taken more than once or in different directions. The challenge is that the handler must direct the dog around the course within the time limits determined by the judge.

Contacts

When agility enthusiasts talk about contact problems, they are not discussing corrective lenses. The dog walk, A-frame, and seesaw are named the contact obstacles because they have a safety zone of thirty-six to forty-two inches, which the dog must touch before completing the obstacle. This zone is usually painted yellow, although other colors are occasionally seen. In all agility associations, the dog must make contact with that zone in order to perform that obstacle correctly.

The *dog walk* resembles a downed tree in the woods. It has an up ramp and a down ramp suspending a level center plank. The confident dog can trot or gallop across this span while maintaining his balance.

The *A-frame* is the largest piece of agility equipment. The original A-frames, resembling obstacles borrowed from police dog training, since have been refined to become more dog friendly while showing off the athleticism of even the smallest dog.

The *seesaw* or *teeter-totter*, as it is sometimes called, is similar to those seen in many children's playgrounds. The dog must tip the board and continue to the end of the plank.

When training is started for these contact obstacles, the dog usually is very careful and will easily touch the safety zone. As the dog develops confidence and increases his speed, he soon discovers that it is faster to do a part of the obstacle, jump off, and continue to the next challenge.

If the dog jumps off the obstacle before touching the contact zone, he has failed and will not receive any credit towards a title on that run. In all agility organizations around the world, the dog cannot get a qualifying score and advance unless he gets a portion of a paw inside that zone. It's the universal agility rule: miss a contact, miss a Q!

Tunnels

Another set of obstacles in agility consists of tunnels. They add excitement to an agility course because the dog is momentarily out of sight of the handler.

The *open tunnel* is often the very first obstacle taught to the dog, and very quickly the dog learns that agility is a fun sport. The original tunnels were made from mine ducting that was used to provide oxygen to miners. Originally tunnels were only available in red or yellow. Today there is a wide range of colors available. Tunnel lengths, which vary from twelve to twenty feet, are secured with sandbags or other holders to prevent them from moving. The tunnels can be straight, curved, S-shaped, or any combination of those shapes.

Chris Miel's Piper, MACH Cross Creek Swatch of Pebwin—blasting out of the tunnel
Photo: Peter Stewart

The *collapsed tunnel* is also called the chute or the blind tunnel. It consists of a solid barrel or entrance with non-skid footing, three feet long. Attached to that is a cloth chute made from lightweight material about six to eight feet in length. The dog must enter the barrel and push through the cloth chute. Many dogs learn this skill as puppies playing with towels and sheets. You will see photographs of goldens exiting this obstacle with big smiles and bouncing feet.

Jumps

The very heart and soul of agility is the jump. The dog is expected to know many types of jumps, and they are set in a variety of patterns to challenge the dog and handler. All jumps are either *"winged"* or *"non-winged."* Similar to horse show jumps, they can take on some interesting shapes and designs. The non-winged jumps consist of two uprights made from wood, PVC, plastic, or metal and an adjustable jump bar. Winged jumps consist of an upright with a frame usually about two feet in width. There are many creative forms of winged jumps consisting of cutouts of dogs or interesting fabrics with club names or logos. Made from PVC pipe, the jump bar for all traditional jumps is about four to five feet long and adjustable in height from four to twenty-six inches.

Chris Miel's Buck, Cross Creek's Broke the Bank, OA, NAJ over the jump. Note that Buck is looking ahead for his next obstacle.   Photo: Peter Stewart

There are specialty jumps such as a *panel jump*, which gives the impression of a solid wall; a *tire jump*, which is a lightweight tire (most are made with four-inch diameter black drainage hose and then taped with bright colors) with an inside diameter of twenty-four inches suspended from a frame; and a *broad jump*, which is made from six- or eight-inch boards raised slightly off the ground.

Mature goldens jump either twenty or twenty-four inches, depending on their shoulder heights. Puppies are started with the jump bars on the ground or at four inches and are gradually moved up as they reach adult height and weight.

Early jump training does not need any fancy equipment. Puppies and young dogs should only jump very low; two bricks and a broomstick will work just fine. As the dog gets older, you can progress to two five-gallon buckets and a broomstick. All the fancy moves such as "cross in front," "cross behind," "reverse flow pivot," "rock back," "left," "right," and virtually anything else can be taught on this very basic equipment.

Weave Poles

The *weave poles* obstacle consists of a series of 1¼-inch PVC poles spaced about twenty-two inches apart. The dog must enter the poles on his left shoulder and proceed to weave in and out until there are no more poles. In competition, you will see between six and twelve poles. There is also a special competition called the *sixty-weave pole challenge* whereby the dog must weave sixty poles in a row. Many people consider this a very difficult obstacle for the dog. Golden retrievers usually learn weave poles quickly and can do this obstacle with amazing speed and grace. Because of the need for the dog to bend around the poles, training for this obstacle should not begin until the dog is at least a year and one-half old. Too much early training may cause problems as the dog matures.

Buck working his way through the weave poles   *Photo: Peter Stewart*

Pause Table

The *pause table* is a table three feet in diameter with a nonskid surface. The dog must climb on the table, which for golden retrievers is set to either sixteen or twenty-four inches, and assume a sit or a down position and hold it while the judge counts out five seconds. This sounds simple, but many dogs don't like the wait and would rather keep moving. When the judge says "go," the contestant continues on his course to the finish line.

Agility Trials

When you go to an agility competition, the dogs are divided into classes depending on their experience. In AKC agility, for instance, dogs begin in Novice, proceed to Open, and then enter the Excellent and finally the Masters level. The courses that the dogs are asked to run become increasingly more difficult, and the rules become stricter. In novice, for example, the dog does not have to be perfect. Several mistakes are allowed. The dog must be able to demonstrate the ability to jump and perform the obstacles on a fairly straightforward course. Agility courses are a timed event. As you and the dog become more experienced, you are expected to complete the course in less time and with fewer mistakes. You are given a course diagram with the day's course drawn out showing where the obstacles are going to be placed and the sequence of obstacles for that day.

Once the course is built, you are permitted to walk the course without your dog. This ritual is called the walk-through. There is where the handlers plan their strategy and run their imaginary dog. Many people get lost in thought as they are trying to memorize the course. Once walk-throughs are completed, the competition begins. When it is your turn on course, you get to the start line, hand over your leash, and when the timer is ready, you direct your dog around the course using verbal and hand signals and body language. You are not permitted to touch your dog.

The elements that make this sport exciting are speed and accuracy. It takes a dog who easily accepts teamwork and pairs that with athletic ability. Golden retrievers enjoy the companionship and physical activity of the sport and take to agility naturally.

How to Get Started

All this equipment sounds very interesting, but how do you get your dog started? Before you begin, you need to make certain you have taught your dog some basic obedience commands or manners. The dog must have a reliable recall. In other words, the dog must come when called. A steady sit, down, and stay are also essential as the very basics of being able to direct and control your dog. Most agility training is done off-leash, so it is important that your early lessons be conducted in a secure area for the dog's safety.

While agility training can begin at any age, the groundwork should ideally begin by about one year of age. A very important consideration is the type of collar and leash used in training. Because agility obstacles have corners, a good fitting flat buckle collar or quick release collar is mandatory. Chains, chokes, and prong collars are not acceptable because the dog can get caught on the edge of a piece of equipment causing either serious injury or death. Retractable leashes are also not a good choice, because they can catch on jumps and entangle the dogs. A good quality cotton web leash is the most comfortable for the handler and advised for the dog's safety.

Dog agility can be a strenuous sport for the dog and handler, so you want to be careful to not overtax growing joints. Dogs have critical growth plates, which can be damaged by excess pounding and physical stress. These growth plates remain open until the dog is approximately eighteen to twenty-two months of age. For the golden puppy, you have an average of 1½ years before you can even think of competing. Two years is even more typical. Our general rule of thumb for golden retrievers is that they jump no higher than the height of their pasterns until they are about six months of age (no higher than eight inches) and elbow height until they are at least fourteen months of age (about twelve inches). Starting at eighteen months of age, you can gradually raise the jumps until they are twenty or twenty-four inches high.

Balance is another aspect of the sport that can prove to be challenging for a puppy who seems to grow inches in just one short day. Basic agility training can take anywhere from eight weeks to two years. It takes the average dog only eight weeks to master most agility obstacles. Most of your training will be focused on getting you to the right place at the right time in order to efficiently and successfully direct your dog around a course. You have a lot of time to do it right and keep the dog happy. The reward is a very close bond between dog and handler and a dog who is fit, well muscled, and happy to work.

Now It's Time to Begin Training

First of all, don't be in a rush. Second, bring your sense of humor. Third, remember that growing bones should not be stressed. Step one in agility training is trust. You will be introducing lots of new commands, tasks, and movements to your puppy, some that he will do willingly and others that will take a little more coaxing. You want to have the puppy look forward to training sessions as an adventure—one in which you will coax him to great efforts where he will succeed and not be frightened. Establishing trust at a very young age will make all your future training much easier.

There are many agility training centers in the United States. Many dog clubs have added agility to the classes they offer. How do you know if the class is a good one for you and your dog?

When you select an agility school, you should visit one or two classes of different levels and observe how the class is being conducted. Are the dogs having fun? Are the handlers having fun? Does the instructor appear knowledgeable? And most importantly, is the training you observe full of praise for the dog?

Agility training does not involve any harsh corrections. The dog is being asked to perform some difficult tasks and is always to be praised for his efforts. Remember that because most training is done off leash, you need to have some basic obedience skills before you begin. The dog must come to you when called and should know how to sit and lie down on command. The instructor should be willing to spend time reassuring a timid dog and should be adept at creating games to teach the basic skills. The emphasis should be on communication between the dog and handler with lots of rewards for a job well done. The Internet is a great source of information on agility including listings of agility trainers, schools, and clubs at www.cleanrun.com and at www.dogpatch.org/agility/. Follow the links to the agility information center. See the Appendix for complete information on accessing resources.

Tracking

Ed and Marallyn Wight

Ed and Marallyn Wight began tracking in 1972 with their first golden retrievers and continue to enjoy the sport both as handlers and judges. Ed's first golden, Kyrie Genever Am/Can UDTDX, WC, was the incentive for the Ann Arbor Dog Training Club's Order of the Muddy Sneaker, and Marallyn's Anthea of Setherwood Am/Can UDTDX was the first golden to earn a Canadian TDX. Between them, the Wights have earned twelve TDX titles in the United States and Canada and have passed numerous TD tests.

Ed has been a tracking judge since 1977, and Marallyn began judging in 1979. Their judging assignments have taken them from coast to coast in the United States, as well as to the Canadian provinces of Ontario and Quebec.

In addition to working their own dogs, the Wights have taught obedience and tracking classes for many years for the Ann Arbor Dog Training Club where they are members. On occasion, they have presented weekend tracking clinics in California, New York, Ohio, and Michigan. They wrote the tracking column for the *Golden Retriever News* for seventeen years. They are members of the Marshbanks Golden Retriever Club of Michigan, as well as the Golden Retriever Club of America.

Ed recently received the national American Kennel Club Community Achievement Award. He is retired from the practice of general dentistry; he has also been a math and science teacher, as well as a high school wrestling coach. Marallyn is retired as a speech and language pathologist in an intermediate school district and has also been a supervising teacher for the University of Michigan.

As judges, Ed's and Marallyn's goal, whenever possible, is to design fair but challenging tracks that they would enjoy having their own goldens run.

U-CDX Kyrie Caerfilly Ngaio, UDTDX, TDX, WC, Can CDX, CGC
Owned, loved and trained by Edwin and Marallyn Wight

As a novice owner of a golden retriever, you will discover it is such fun to find that they are so adaptable! If your interests lie in showing your dog in the breed ring, obedience trials, tracking tests, hunting tests, field trials, or agility events, your new special friend can accomplish much in many of these areas. Of course, if you're just interested in owning a "couch potato," that can probably also be arranged, although it is much kinder to introduce your golden to at least one of these activities. Surprise! You may find that you get hooked and continue for your sake, as well as that of your dog's!

Do you like being outdoors? Are you interested in enjoyable exercise for you as well as for your golden? Then you may well appreciate the bonding that tracking will develop for you and your dog. What is tracking? How can you tell if your golden will take to it?

Ability to Recognize and Follow Human Scent

According to the American Kennel Club's Tracking Regulations, "The purpose of a tracking test is to demonstrate the dog's ability to recognize and follow human scent, a skill that is useful in the service of mankind." There are four tracking titles and certificates available from the AKC: Tracking Dog (TD), Tracking Dog Excellent (TDX), Variable Surface Tracker (VST), and Champion Tracker (CT). How to earn those coveted titles will be outlined later. The Canadian Kennel Club offers the Tracking Dog and Tracking Dog Excellent titles; their tests are similar to those of the AKC and also will be described later.

Born to Track

To answer the question about the golden retriever's interest in and ability for tracking, it is indeed rare to find one that doesn't have these aptitudes. A look at the annual statistics for tracking titles awarded in the United States finds that golden retrievers generally rank number one of all breeds in earning those titles. The majority of goldens love the outdoors and the "games" they can play there.

We're often asked if males or females are better trackers; we've put multiple titles on both sexes, so we think it's an individual matter. Males, of course, often want to "mark" bushes, trees, etc., but if you inhibit that from the start, it shouldn't be a problem. We've never had that with our males; they've been too interested in the track!

When to Begin

We particularly like to teach the basics of tracking to puppies and have generally started ours informally when they are about ten weeks old. Puppies are curious; they like to investigate their environment, and, of course, they're low to the ground, so they're automatically using their noses!

This is not to say that older dogs can't be taught to track; they certainly can have more singleness of purpose than puppies, who can be distractible. However, puppies have that marvelous curiosity and interest in the world, so appropriately controlled tracking lessons (suitable length and difficulty) are one of the best activities for them. Have you tried hiding from your puppy? Have you tried hiding one of its favorite toys? Do one of these activities, and you may well see your pup using nose as well as eyes to find you or that toy.

With beginners, we start by having someone hold the puppy or dog, wearing a buckle collar, on a six-foot lead. The owner leaves and moves a medium distance over low cover and then a shorter distance into longer cover where he or she can't be seen. (The owner then may call the pup's name if it isn't watching.) The puppy or dog is probably straining at the leash to get to its owner, so the second person hurries out as soon as the owner is hidden. The owner should really praise the dog or puppy when he or she is reached. Praise at this point is usually enough reward, although a "goodie" later may be additional motivation. Try this two or three times, with each trip into the high cover, but quit while the puppy or dog is still eager to continue.

Hiding Toys

If you want to try hiding a toy for your golden to find in the house, let it watch the first time or two while you put the toy behind some furniture. Do this just three or four times at each endeavor, letting the puppy search free, without collar or lead. Again, quit while you're ahead! Always use the same name for the toy when you encourage your puppy to "find" it. Eventually, you can keep your puppy or dog out of sight while you hide the object; let it search as soon as you've hidden the object.

We still do this occasionally with our trained dogs, particularly when we can't lay a regular track for them. This is a great game for them, too, and it's just another way for them to use their noses.

We do other activities with our goldens and enjoy them all, but tracking really is our first love. In addition to the fact that both we and our dogs enjoy it as an activity, we agree wholeheartedly with another quote from the American Kennel Club Regulations:

"Tracking, by nature, is a vigorous, noncompetitive out-door sport. Tracking tests demonstrate the willingness and enjoyment of the dog in its work, and should always represent the best in sportsmanship and camaraderie by the people involved."

This is very true. Because everyone involved in tracking realizes the effort and dedication involved in earning tracking titles, all are genuinely happy to see a dog successfully complete a test. There are no scores involved; it is "Pass" or "Fail," and congratulations for a job well done are sincere.

How to Get Started

How to get started? Naturally, it helps if you can find a tracking class in your area or someone who has tracked before who is willing to help you. There are also several publications on the market that can give you the steps to follow. If you are anywhere in the area of clubs that have tracking tests, contact them to see when they have a test scheduled, particularly the beginning level TD test. Observers are welcome (without their dogs), and someone there will always be willing to answer your questions. You'll also see why we say everyone is happy to see a dog pass; it's a great feeling!

The events calendar of the American Kennel Club lists tracking tests along with other schedules. You should also contact the AKC for a copy of the tracking regulations. See Appendix—AKC.

Single copies of the regulations are free, and they go into more detail about what is required to earn the various tracking titles.

If you can't locate a tracking class in your area or an experienced tracker who can help, perhaps you can persuade another beginner to meet and practice with you. Humans that we are, it is much easier to work by pairing up with someone else than it is to do it alone!

What Kind of Equipment Is Needed for Tracking?

To begin with, have your puppy or dog on a plain buckle collar and a six-foot lead. Later you will need a forty-foot lead and a tracking harness, but it isn't advisable to start with those at first. (As is true with other dog activities, it is the handler who needs at least as much training as the animal, and this is particularly true when it comes to handling a forty-foot lead.) Harnesses and leads can be purchased through dog equipment companies or can even be made by the owner. (Our first puppy harness was made of half-inch wide cotton webbing and pop rivets.)

Leads

Leads should be twenty to, preferably, forty feet long and can be made of cotton or nylon webbing, or cord, the thickness of the latter depending on the strength and size of the dog.

Harnesses

Harnesses should be "straps of plain, pliable material," and should be non-restrictive, in other words, not binding the shoulders. If a harness is described as being for tracking, it should be acceptable. If they bind the shoulders, pulling or roading harnesses are probably not acceptable. If the harness is adjustable, it will be particularly useful for a growing dog.

Non-restrictive tracking harness

Stakes

You will need stakes to mark the start of your tracks and the corners (or turns) as you get further in your training. Bicycle flags or narrow dowels can be used for these, with the ends sharpened so they'll stick into the ground. If you use dowels, attach some surveyor's tape to the top so you can see the stakes from a distance. We prefer not to use metal stakes because we often practice in farm fields and don't want to leave anything behind which might damage farm machinery. It is a good idea to count the number of stakes one has used, to be sure all are collected when one is through. Start accumulating *old socks, slippers, gloves,* etc., to use as tracking articles.

(You may want to start the game with that favorite toy, but you'll soon want to change over to what might be used in a test.) The article to find in a TD test is either a *glove* or a *wallet*. We'll talk later about the articles in TDX and VST tests. We'll also mention some other minor equipment you may find useful.

Boots and Clothing

Boots and weather-appropriate clothing for you are also advisable. If you have a strong-pulling golden, you may want gloves so that you don't get leash burns, although this shouldn't be a factor with a puppy.

Where to Practice?

The best place for practice depends on the part of the country in which you live. Public parks are possible, as are state recreation areas, depending upon local regulations. In rural areas, fallow farm fields are a possibility. In asking for permission to use land, we always explain that our dogs are on lead and under control, and, of course, we're very careful to leave everything as we found it. Sometimes it helps to explain tracking as being similar to search and rescue, in case "tracking" has been misunderstood as "trapping."

Variable Surface Tracking involves more urban areas than do the TD and TDX tests, but we'll discuss that later.

From now on, we'll refer just to tracking with a puppy, although what we suggest applies to the novice adult dog as well. We have said that beginning lessons should be done with your pup on a six-foot lead and wearing a buckle collar. The buckle collar, rather than an obedience collar, is preferred because we use no physical corrections in tracking. Much later, when the puppy knows the game, we may then use a verbal reminder or admonition only if necessary to stop some "fooling around." A six-foot lead is easier for the handler to use until he or she has a feel for the game.

You may start using a harness after two or three lessons with the collar. When you begin to use the longer lead, you'll still want to keep the distance short between you and the puppy, letting the extra length trail behind you on the ground. (Letting out more lead can begin when your puppy is into the game, is staying on the track, and is really pulling down it.) Walk the puppy to the start of the track with the lead on its collar; change it to the harness only when you are ready to track. Then when you are finished (at the article), transfer the leash back to the collar again. This eventually is a signal of, "Now I'm tracking; now I'm not."

Ed Wight and U-CDX Kryie Miss Christie, Am/Can CDX, TD, Can TDX

How Often to Practice?

Frequency of practice, naturally, depends on your lifestyle, but we suggest three to four regular lessons a week, with two to three "runs" each time. Always quit while your pup is still interested and really wants to do more. Remember, no corrections at this time, but lots of praise when your dog gets to the article. Act as though it's the greatest thing in the world to have found something! Your pup may not retrieve at this point, but play with the article, throw it up in the air, etc. Eventually the puppy may retrieve, but if not, you can always later teach the puppy to sit or go down at the article. Tracking regulations state that the test article may be either retrieved or indicated.

How We Begin

Because there is more than one good method of teaching dogs to track, and this is not really a training manual, we aren't going into details of how we teach dogs to track. We will comment about how we begin, however.

1. With the on-lead puppy watching from behind a starting stake, the "tracklayer" will shuffle step about ten yards, put in another stake, turn to face the puppy and handler, call the pup's name while waving the article, drop it in the vicinity of the stake, and return a few feet out on another line to the handler. The handler will let the puppy go as

fast as it wants to the article. Much praise for even noticing the article! (Better for the handler not to talk too much while the puppy is tracking, however; we want its attention on the track, not on the handler.)

2. The same procedure is repeated, starting beyond where the second stake was and moving both stakes so that the line is a bit longer for the second run. Again, the tracklayer shuffle steps; this takes the place of "double laying" the track. The puppy may want to run to the article, which is very good at this point; it can be slowed down later when it knows the game. At any time it pulls off to the side, the handler simply stops until the pup comes back to the line. Of course, on these early short tracks, the puppy is probably mainly using its eyes. Relying on its nose will come later with experience and longer tracks.

3. We would repeat this procedure about three times, depending upon the pup's interest, extending the length of each run about five additional yards. At the next lesson, we might have the first run as long as the last one at the previous lesson. We may also find that a "goodie" with the article makes the game even more intriguing, although during summer "bug time," we have to be sure that insects don't find the tidbit before the pup does.

Make a Map

Get into the habit of making maps of your practice tracks; when you can, have two features lined up for "double sighting" so you know you're walking a straight line. It's embarrassing, in addition to being nonproductive, if you insist your puppy goes a different way than it wants to, and then you find it's right, and you're wrong! Even when the puppy can do multiple corners or turns, with the track aged as in a TD test, we do not make it regulation length until the puppy is mature enough for that. Again, if you possibly can, go to watch a tracking test, or watch other dogs in practice; very often it helps to learn to "read" our own animal's tracking behavior by observing that of others.

*Marallyn Wight and U-CD Kyrie Havin'A Celidh, Am/Can CD
"Ready for her first tracking test."*

In Conclusion

This section isn't meant to be a training manual. However, we do have some final thoughts that may be of help, whether or not you ever enter any tracking events.

▼ Be familiar with the rules.

▼ Build from the beginning and don't be afraid to go back in your training if your pup is having a problem.

▼ Follow a plan; be consistent in your training. Observe others, and don't be afraid to ask for help.

▼ Remember the importance of appropriate praise; necessary corrections (only after the pup knows the game) should be minimal and verbal only.

▼ Be sure that you know exactly where your practice track is, so that you're not restraining your dog wrongly.

▼ Make maps; mark your turns not just with stakes, but use alternative markers as well, short dowels, clips, clothespins, etc. (Use something you can see, but that isn't that apparent to the pup from a distance.)

▼ Above all, be sure that tracking is fun for both you and your golden. Whether or not you ever enter a test, tracking is one of the best ways we know to bond with that delightful fur ball you've welcomed into your family.

Obedience

Connie Cleveland

Connie Cleveland grew up at Heron Acres Golden Retrievers. She entered the showring for the first time at eight years of age, earning her first championship title with Ch. Shawn's Golden Boomerang UDTX when she was twelve years old. By the time she reached college, Connie was teaching obedience classes in her spare time, and shortly after college, she became the director of a program that trained service dogs to assist the physically disabled, a line of work that has continued for a decade. Her many obedience achievements include five Obedience Trial champions, two Gaines-Cycle golden dumbbells, a UDT Maltese, and a CDX Shih Tzu.

Since founding Dog Trainers Workshop, the Clevelands have worked with more than seven thousand owner/dog teams, coaching many to wins in obedience, agility, and tracking. Using the Clevelands' balanced approach to motivation and compulsion, hundreds of students have earned obedience titles including many OTCCh, UD, and UDX titles.

Cleveland students have gained national recognition in National Specialties, the Eastern and Central Regional Gaines/Cycle competitions, and many Obedience Trial championships with perfect scores of 200.

See Appendix—video for Connie's video collection—*Dogs Are Problem Solvers: Complete Obedience Training—The Connie Cleveland Method.*

Basic Obedience

All dogs need training for good manners. However, some of the most typical behavior problems in golden retrievers can be easily predicted because of their personality. Typical complaints include:

▼ "He pulls on a leash whenever he sees another person or dog." In this case, his outgoing and inquisitive nature gets him in trouble!

"OFF" is an important command to teach your Golden. Jessie, age 3, demonstrates the hand signal for the command "OFF".

Photo: Cannon Goodnight

▼ "He jumps on my guests." Again, his outgoing nature causes trouble!

▼ "He is picking up everything that is laying around our house and yard." In this instance, his natural desire to retrieve causes the problem! Let's begin with some basics so that you can enjoy your golden for many, many years.

Pulling on a Leash

A dog with poor manners on a leash believes that if he wants to go east, he should just pull east, as hard as it takes to drag his owner along with him. You can easily communicate to your dog that pulling you will not make you follow him.

▼ Stand with him on a collar and leash. Imagine that you have a circle, the radius of the leash, around you. If your dog tries to drag you out of that circle, give a quick tug on the leash. When you tug, if he turns and looks at you, praise him. However, if he just stops pulling and doesn't look, that's OK, but save your praise for when he is paying attention.

▼ Don't be surprised if he immediately starts pulling in a different direction! In his mind, something grabbed on the neck when he ran east, so he may try west! He will not immediately generalize and learn that pulling in any direction is wrong. There is no need to become angry at your dog for pulling you. Let him discover the natural consequence of his action.

▼ If he pulls, you will tug (other words for this procedure are "pop" or "jerk.") Tugging is simply a rapid jerk on the leash with equally rapid release. The tug should be appropriate to the age and size of the dog. Do not be emotional or think he's dumb. Stay calm, and when he looks at you, respond with lots of praise (and treats if you like), whether his attention is due to his anxiety, frustration, or excitement.

▼ Try standing in different locations. Just because he will not try to pull you in the front yard, does not mean that he will remember not to pull on a different side of the house. When the location changes, so do the distractions! Finally, after numerous locations, your dog will generalize and understand that, "No matter where I am, when I pull, the consequence is the same, therefore, I will not pull on the leash."

Walking on a leash

When your dog can stand on a loose leash, it is time to teach him to walk on a loose leash.

▼ Start walking, and give your dog a command that means, "Let's go for a walk." (i.e. "Let's go.") Don't worry about whether your dog is on your left or right side. It does *Flexi Lead courtesy of PetEdge* not matter. He is not heeling; he is simply being polite as he walks on the leash. If your dog pulls on the leash, give a tug. If he looks at you when you tug the leash, praise him. If you have trouble getting your dog to stop pulling with a tug on the leash, give a tug, and turn and walk in the opposite direction. Changing direction will clearly tell your dog that you are not going in the direction that he is pulling! Soon he will be walking on a loose leash with you, sometimes looking at you, sometimes looking around, but always aware enough to stop when you stop and change direction when you do.

▼ All dogs must learn that pulling on their owner's leash is unacceptable. Often, a dog that pulls his owner along on a leash, especially as he strains to get to another person or dog, will start to bark and lunge and act aggressively. This is true of all breeds, not just goldens. Restraining your dog will actually increase his excitement and aggression! It is imperative that you don't ever have to restrain your dog. He can look around and sniff, but he should never strain at the end of the leash to go where he desires.

Coming When Called

The command, "Come," is only useful when it stops a dog that is running away, chasing something, or is distracted. When your dog can stand on a loose leash and walk on a loose leash, it's time for him to learn to come when you call.

You will need a long line or leash fifteen to twenty feet in length.

*Cotton Web Long Line
courtesy of PetEdge*

▼ Begin by holding the end of the line, and let your dog wander around. When he is sufficiently distracted by something, call his name and command "come." If he does not obey, give enough of a tug on the rope to get his attention, then back up, encouraging him to come to you. Once again, the tug on the rope means, "pay attention to me!" Your dog will want to avoid the tug on the rope, so he will respond to this training in one of two ways. He will either come every time you call him, or he will stop being distracted and will stay close to you even though he is on his long line. It is time to move on to the next step.

▼ Take him for a walk, and let him drag the rope. When he becomes distracted, call his name and say, "come." If he does not come, pick up the rope, and give a tug, making him come. As he is coming, you *back up* to the spot where you were standing when you initially called him. It's time for him to learn that after *one* command to come, you will enforce it. When your dog is coming every time you call him while dragging a long rope, start using a shorter rope. Let him drag four to six feet of line instead of fifteen to twenty feet. You will still be able to go get him and make him come when he does not.

There is one thing worse than a dog that does not come when called and that is a dog that runs away. You will know when you can trust your dog to come without a line, not because he is perfect every time you call him when he drags the line, but because every time he sees you coming toward him, he starts toward you. This is an indication that he has learned that running away from you is ineffective, but coming toward you is a right response. You will find that even off leash, if he fails to come, and you start toward him, he will move toward you and not away!

Goldens are famous for picking up items around the house and running with them. There is nothing wrong with attaching a rope or leash to a puppy or dog when he is in the house and letting him drag it. When he picks up an item that you wish he did not have, call him to you. If he does not come, go get the rope or leash and make him come. When he comes to you, pet him, praise him, and then take the object from him. It is important that you are not angry when you catch him, but very matter of fact. You told him to come and he did not, so you caught him, and made him come. Soon, he will realize that you call him whenever he picks something up, so instead of running, he will start bringing the object to you. Furthermore, he will soon lose interest in picking everything up because it does not cause you to chase him.

Getting in a Crate or Kennel

Not long ago, I was doing some basic obedience with a young dog that did not belong to me. About the fourth day I realized that getting him back in the crate in my van was a problem when it was his turn to get in. Instead, he would go under the van or just circle the van. "Kennel" became the lesson for the day. I simply put him on a leash and asked him to jump into and back out of his crate repeatedly. I happily gave him a treat and a loving pat after he had kenneled, but I did not use the treat to bribe him into the van. He had a leash attached to him, and if I asked him to kennel and he did not, I simply pulled him in. Again, there were no negative emotions. It was my expectation that he would get in, and in less than ten repetitions, he would happily jump in his crate when asked.

Good Behavior

Does your dog bark when people come to your door?

▼ Put a squirt bottle of water near your door, and set it on a jet stream. When there is a knock on the door, go to the door with him, encouraging him to bark by saying, "speak" or "who's there." When you get to the door, tell him "quiet." If he does not stop, squirt him. (Goldens like water, so it may take two or three quick squirts for him to be offended.) Praise him for being quiet, and then let in your guest.

When the guest comes in, is your dog going to jump on him?

▼ You can use your squirt bottle to teach him that the foyer is off limits when you give him the command "get back." Begin by pretending that you are leaving the house. When he follows you enthusiastically to the door, tell him to "get back" and move towards him as you squirt him out of the foyer. Walk out without him. Wait a few seconds, and walk back in. If he runs up to jump on you, chase him back out of the foyer by squirting him with the water. When he has backed up out of the foyer, go to him and pet him.

▼ When he understands that he must "get back" when you command, then it is time to ask a friend to come to practice with you. Have your friend knock on the door. Go to the door with your dog, tell him "get back," and if necessary, squirt him to move him out of the foyer. Then let your friend in. If he enthusiastically runs up to greet him, tell him "get back" and again squirt him to move him out of the foyer. Repeat this process as many times as necessary until he learns that when people are at the door, he may run to the door to meet them, but not enter the foyer to jump on them.

Other Common Behavior Problems

Does your dog steal food off your counters?

▼ Put out a sheet of clear contact paper, sticky side up, and leave the room. Natural consequences teach some tough lessons! You get on my counters, and you will be in a really sticky mess.

If you are holding a plate on your lap or have a snack on a coffee table, will your dog try to snatch a bite for himself?

▼ This is easily remedied by reacting to his thievery just as an older dog would if a younger dog tried to steal a bone or toy. Next time he reaches for a bite, make an exclamation mimicking an older dog's growl (i.e., "No," or, "Hey"), and make a quick movement toward your dog. Moving toward him is mimicking the snap that an older dog would make to defend what is his. Your correction should be quick, loud, and businesslike. Dogs are that way when correcting one another, and you can be the same.

Is your dog apt to steal items out of the trash?

▼ Put a mousetrap in the top of the almost-full wastebasket, and cover with a paper towel. The purpose is not for your dog to be hurt by the trap, but to have the wastebasket explode. A warning: you must be home when this happens so that you can reset the trap; otherwise your dog will regain his courage and discover that if he quickly bumps the wastebasket, it only explodes once, and then he can eat the trash! Remember, doing this in one wastebasket will keep him out of that wastebasket, but not any others until he has had similar experiences in a variety of wastebaskets.

Jumping Up

Most young puppies begin jumping up as soon as they realize they can get their feet in your lap whenever you are sitting. There is nothing wrong with a dog that jumps up if he is invited, but he should also get "off" when asked.

▼ While sitting in the chair, tell him "off," and if he does not put four feet back on the floor, put your foot on one of his back feet. Feeling pressure on his back foot, he will perceive that he is trapped and get off. Praise him and repeat the process when he climbs up again.

▼ You can use the same technique with a dog that is big enough to try to put his feet on your table or counter. The same correction is appropriate. Tell him "off," and then gently step on his back foot. It won't be long before he understands the command means "put four feet back on the floor."

Nothing is more enjoyable than a well-mannered golden retriever. Start with the basics and prepare to enjoy his company for many, many years.

Learning To Pay Attention

Apply this to teaching your dog that a POP on the leash (a negative reinforcement) means "pay attention to me" (the desired response). Teaching a dog to pay attention is crucial to any type of training. None of us would attempt to teach a child who was not paying attention; apply the same rule to your dog.

Beth, 3 months old, is learning to pay attention   Photo: Sylvia Donahey-Feeney

Pay Attention

Tell your dog to sit while standing in front of him. It is much easier for dogs to look up from a front position than from a heel position, but heel position is only a few steps away! Position the leash under his chin. Use any type of collar you like; it depends completely upon the dog, his temperament, and his age. If you are training a puppy, a simple buckle or snap nylon collar is best.

Begin by bribing him with a treat. Hold the treat in your hand (or mouth if you prefer) with the leash between his face and your face. You must believe that your dog is physically capable of looking at you. You also want him to believe that looking at you is physically possible for him to do. At this point, the dog can make eye contact. When he is looking at you, talk to him, and praise him with your voice (not your hands; they are busy holding onto the leash). CAREFUL. If he looks away—stop talking. He is only a "good boy" when he is looking. Praise for exactly what you want—in this case—looking at you.

Ready? Next time he looks away, pop the leash straight up. How hard? The dog should indicate that he felt it. Your correction should offend the dog.

Responses

Now here is the hard part. You must take control of the dog's response. What are the responses the dog can give you?

To jump up out of his sit. Your dog is offended by the correction and is trying to solve the problem that the leash correction gives him. Getting up is a pretty good guess on your dog's part. After all, maybe he thinks a pop on the leash means MOVE. You respond by pushing him back into a sit and lifting his head up with your hands. Then praise him for looking even though you are making him do it. Your attitude needs to be "good guess, wrong answer"; try this instead.

Sucking his head and neck into his shoulders as if to say, "Okay, boss, I'll brace myself for the next one." Again, he is acting as if he is offended. You respond by tapping the top of his head with a finger or lifting his head up. Show him how to respond, then praise the response. He's looking up at you; PRAISE HIM.

No response at all? If you did not jerk hard enough, then your correction is not something the dog cares about stopping. It is not offensive to your dog. Be careful! Use brains not brawn. A harder jerk is not always the answer. Certainly there are some dogs that would not even notice you were jerking unless they were wearing a pinch collar around their neck, but there are others who get a glazed over look in their eye and do nothing at all in order to "save themselves." Popping harder on this type of dog will result in a very confused and fearful dog. Ultimately your goal is to see the two most important parts about the correction become clear to your dog. He has learned how to stop the correction and demonstrates this by looking up at you without hesitation when you POP the leash. He has learned how to avoid the correction and demonstrates this by looking away less and less, until even with distractions he will not take his eyes off you.

Changing Position

Now you can change your position relative to the dog. Stand at a ninety-degree angle to him, as if he had just swung his rear out and done an extremely crooked sit. When he understands how to stop and avoid the correction in this position, try standing in the heel position.

Remember, you are not just teaching your dog to sit in heel position and look at you; you are teaching him a correction. He must understand how to control that correction. If he understands both how to stop and how to avoid the POP on the leash, you have accomplished an important prerequisite for teaching heeling with attention.

Correcting Your Dog

Many years ago at my first obedience class, I trudged around the ring with my Maltese in tow (literally) and was informed that any time my dog was out of position, (forging, lagging, sitting when he was not supposed to sit, not sitting when he should, sniffing, etc.) that I should correct him. A correction was simply a jerk on the leash in the direction I wanted the dog to move, i.e., up, back, in, out. I still have nightmares about that poor dog. How in the world did he stand it? His every move was met with a jerk—followed by praise. "Correct and praise" was the class motto. Praise for what? The best thing that dog could hope to understand was that he was good for allowing me to jerk his neck.

Thankfully, dog training has become much more sophisticated for me. I do not randomly jerk on a dog's neck, and I only praise for behavior that I like. A leash correction has a very specific meaning for my dogs; it means *look at me*. If I give a POP on my leash, it means my dog is not paying attention to me. I expect my dog to understand the correction. To understand the correction, whether it be a leash jerk, an ear pinch, a throw chain, or anything the dog finds offensive, the dog must be taught how to respond to the correction. A correction is not a random act of violence; a correction does not evoke terror, fear, or submission—only a right response. A correction is negative reinforcement that the dog knows how to stop and how to avoid.

Teaching a dog how to respond to a correction is a systematic process. If you are successful, your dog will understand the two facts about negative reinforcement:

▼ How to make it stop and
▼ How to avoid it to prevent it from ever happening again.

If your dog understands these two facts, he will not be sullen or sulky; his spirit will not break, because he can completely control whether or not the correction occurs.

Example: An underground fence correction

A simple example of a dog understanding a correction is a dog that is kept in a yard by an "underground fence" (a buried wire that emits a sound or gives a shock when a dog leaves its yard). When a dog is taught this correction properly, he understands two facts:

▼ How to stop the shock (jump back into the yard) and
▼ How to avoid the shock (stay in the yard)

Many owners are thoughtless about introducing their dog to the underground fence. The most common error made is to turn the dog loose in the yard and allow him to run around and "discover" the shock. These owners are surprised when the dog gets shocked and bolts out of the yard. Huge problems result! The dog has discovered the wrong response to the correction—*run fast*; it only hurts for an instant.

Another error when teaching the dog about the underground fence, is to "skip steps" in the training process. For example, if a puppy with no prior leash training is put on a leash and walked up to the boundary, when he feels the correction, he might lie down and refuse to move. In his mind, this new skill—walking on a leash—is dangerous. He associates the leash with the electric correction. The correction that meant "stay in the yard" (it was clear to the owner) meant "walking on a leash is dangerous" (it was equally clear to the puppy). The puppy or dog, must understand leash walking BEFORE the fence's boundary is introduced.

Teach the fence correction simply by leading an already leash-trained dog around the yard with visual boundaries (flags or ropes). When the dog experiences the correction (in this case an electric shock), pull him firmly and gently back into the yard. The dog will soon understand the two facts about the fence's correction:

▼ How to stop the correction—move back into the yard and
▼ How to avoid the correction—stay away from the boundary.

When the owner takes control of the correction and, more importantly, takes control of the dog's response, the underground fence correction can be taught. The same is true for ANY correction, whether given by the environment as in the case of the underground fence, or by the trainer.

Field Training

Jackie Merten

Jackie Mertens's interest in dogs dates back to grade school when she and her cocker spaniel earned a UDT degree in obedience. She successfully showed and titled golden retrievers in conformation and obedience for several years before developing a keen interest in hunting and field events. Since that time, training and competing in Field Trials have been a way of life for Jackie.

Jackie is quite simply one of the most successful amateur retriever trainers and breeders in North America. She has trained and titled numerous FC/AFC retrievers. She is a six-time finalist at the National Open/National Amateur Retriever Championships. She won the National Amateur Championship with her NAFC FC Topbrass Cotton, who is the *all time* high point golden retriever in the breed. Breeding, training, and campaigning retrievers is a way of life for Jackie.

Her Topbrass kennel, established in 1968, consistently produces high quality performance golden retrievers and Labrador retrievers.

Jackie's Video—*Sound Beginnings Retriever Training*—describes in detail a comprehensive and progressive training program for retriever puppies from seven weeks to eight months of age. It can also be used to introduce an adult retriever to the world of retrieving. See the Appendix—Videos for details.

The Three "Ss" Of Puppy Training–Short, Simple, Successful

Acquire your pup at or around seven weeks of age. He needs to interact with his littermates until then, but should be separated from them by eight weeks of age. As soon as you get your pup, start teaching him "how to learn." A seven-week-old pup is very capable of learning. From seven to sixteen weeks of age, pups learn "how to learn." It is a very important time frame in the life of your pup. Use it wisely. Remember, puppies cannot learn anything locked in a crate or left in a dog run. Your pup should become a part of your family and your life.

Duck hunting—Ram River Rave of Topbrass

Early puppy training should be done in small doses with bits of food as rewards—I like to use pieces of cheese (dog kibble or hard treats take too long to chew). Hold a small piece of cheese over his head and say *sit*. When he finally "plops his butt down," say *good* and give him the piece of cheese. This can be done about ten times in a row or until the pup acts bored or distracted. Try to always stop a lesson before the pup gets bored. If you do this two or three times a day, your pup will know the word "sit" in a couple of days. At this point, it is situational training. This means that the pup knows "sit" in this setting but does not really know the word thoroughly, such as if he were outside and you did not hold a reward over his head.

Teach "down" using the same principle. With pup in the sitting position, bring your hand to the floor in front of pup and say "down." He will quickly learn to lie down to get at the tidbit in your hand—praise and release his food reward. It is good for your pup to know the "down" command in order to later lie down quietly in a holding blind or duck blind.

I like to have our pups wear soft leather or nylon collars on their necks soon after they are separated from the litter. After a few days of scratching the collar, they adjust to having it on their neck. At this point, snap a lightweight lead on the collar. Let the pup guide you at first. Do not drag or tug at his neck. Eventually try to guide the pup or coax him into following you with praise, tidbits, and rewards. After several days, the pup should be readily walking on lead. Encourage him with praise and food to stay close to your side. Keep his attention.

Off-Leash Walks

Take your pup off leash for walks in the woods or park. This will introduce him to various cover changes, footing, smells, and sights. Have him wade through puddles, navigate ditches, and negotiate stairs. This also teaches him to follow you. Since he is in a strange place, he is likely to want to stay close to the only thing with which he is familiar—you. This helps bonding and establishes you as the leader. Sometimes, when your pup gets distracted, hide on him or change your position. When he discovers that you are gone, he will probably get a little worried and start whining or looking for something familiar. Now call and coax him to you and pet and praise him—this can help establish you as the leader and the puppy as the follower. You have become his leader and protector.

Darla at 7 weeks of age—off leash in the field
Photo: Cannon Goodnight

Play Fetch

Have your pup fetch rolled-up socks or small puppy bumpers (new paint rollers make ideal puppy bumpers—lightweight, soft, and easy to pick up). Once your pup likes to retrieve, start hand tossing him "bumpers," and coax him to you. Kneel to his level, clap, praise, and move away from him if he hesitates to come. Most young pups will come when they think you are leaving them. If you have an independent pup, you might start his retrieves by using a hallway of your house with the doors closed. This will limit his options. You can reward him with cheese for coming; but he may decide to drop the bumper and run in without it for his cheese treat. Don't worry if this happens; at least he is obeying the "come" or "here" command. If he does not come, you may want to spend a few days on the "come" or "here" command using the treats as a reward before going back to retrieving.

Enroll in a local puppy class. This gets your pup out into the community where he can learn to interact with distractions and other dogs. Go visit several classes if you have a choice—there are good and bad puppy trainers. Choose the class and instructor with whom you feel most comfortable. These classes are often called KPT (Kindergarten Puppy Training).

Rhubarb Pie, 6 months of age, executes a beautiful water entry

Let's Go Swimming

If it is warm (water temperature over 50 degrees), pups can swim at an early age. The easiest way is to wade into the water and coax your pup in with you. *Important:* do not toss or drag the pup in—let him enter on his own. If he won't go in, wait and try again in a couple of days. You might try playing with him and other dogs in and around the water. He will eventually swim; be patient. He may be ten or twelve weeks old before he decides to venture in; don't worry, and don't force the issue.

Add a Helper (Thrower)

When your pup is retrieving your hand-tossed objects (three to four months of age), introduce a thrower to him. Use white or contrasting colored objects that he will see on cut grass or flooring if you are indoors. Have the thrower stand ten or fifteen feet away, "hup hup" to get the pup's attention, and toss the object. Release pup as soon as he wants to go.

Only do three or four retrieves at a time, then put your pup away. Do this once each day or every other day. Note: we do not have puppies retrieve birds until they have been force broken. We "force break" pups at five to eight months of age.

Instead of trying to stretch the distance your pup goes on his retrieves, keep them short so as not to tire him. Only gradually make the retrieves more complicated. Have a little change of cover, run across a mowed path, angle a safe ditch, or cross a large puddle of water (that he won't run around!). Be innovative—put chairs out that he has to run past. Also try having a person stand short of another person who throws, so he runs past the first person en route to the object.

Try to get pup to run at the object and not at the thrower. **Note:** If he is running at the thrower, then the thrower is too far away. Make the distance between you and the thrower shorter and lengthen the actual distance of the throw, so pup runs at the object and not the thrower.

At some point, a pistol shot can replace the "hup hup." It is not that important how you get the pup's attention, but you don't want to startle him with the noise of a gun. Our pups hear guns as soon as they go training with us. They are in our vehicles while we are training the big dogs; so they hear the guns in the distance from seven weeks of age. If you don't have other dogs that you are working, introduce gunshots at a distance, so as not to startle your pup.

When dealing with your pup, remember the three "Ss"— **Short, Simple, Successful!**

Accessories for Retriever Training

Drying Your Dog   For quickly and effectively drying your dog after water work. Get "The Absorber" and use it in place of a towel. It is an artificial chamois that stays wet all the time, does not mildew, and won't rot. If kept in its original tube, it stays moist at all times. It absorbs more and better than a towel, does not have to be dried out, and is easily stored in a small place. We purchased ours at K-Mart.

Stakeout Chains	Get the stakeouts that you screw or push into the ground so you can stake out your dog while you or your training partners are training another dog. The staked out dog gets a chance to stretch his legs or dry out completely (after wiping him off).
Vests	Use the neoprene vests or wet suit for dogs for cold-water work in the fall and winter months or sitting all day in a duck blind. They are very effective at keeping in body heat. Various mail order sporting suppliers sell them.
Marking Birds	Use white streamers on your long birds in a dark background where throws are impossible to see or when training late in the day. We tie them to a leg. We were able to purchase white rolls of engineers tape, but one-inch white ribbon will do. You can also make streamers by tearing strips from old sheets. Tear strips fifteen inches long.
Wingers	Use a Winger to get a flyer effect on your bird. They shoot out the bird or bumper further than any human arm can possibly throw one. The dogs seem to love them as much as a flyer.
Strong Arm	Use the strong arm at stations where you have a poor thrower. It throws high and consistent each time.
Bags	Use the large canvas beanbags from LL Bean to easily carry bumpers and birds. When they are soiled, they can be thrown in the washing machine with bleach, and they come out fine.
Cover	Use a camouflage umbrella for retired guns or cover up with a piece of lightweight camouflage material. Either is easier to use than carrying out a cumbersome holding blind to retire behind.

Evaluating Your Dog Objectively For Advanced Field Work

Many owners think their dog can be a great field competitor. When asked why, they invariably say he loves to carry underwear around the house, always has something in his mouth, loves to play in his water bucket, lays in any puddle he finds, retrieves the family parakeet, or fights the water hose. None of these statements mean anything in terms of potential to compete successfully in the field.

Realistically evaluating your dog's potential to compete in field events takes some time and effort. First, your dog must be obedience trained enough to be under control when not on leash. He must know come, sit, heel, and stay and must retrieve to hand. If you have done some training in the field, the following list should help determine his potential.

▼ Is your dog enthusiastic about coming to line and looking out in the field for thrower stations?

▼ Will he willingly look at a long station and be willing to retrieve when the thrower is two hundred yards away?

▼ Will he retrieve three or four times in a row with equal enthusiasm, or does he lose interest after the first or second retrieve?

Topbrass Rita D Riot marking her bird at a licensed Field Trial

▼ Does he hunt up a bumper with enthusiasm, or is he lackadaisical?

▼ Does he walk on his hunts and get distracted if he doesn't find the bumper in a few seconds?

▼ Does he remember the second bird of a double? When he returns with the first retrieve, does he come back to line and eagerly look for the second thrower station?

▼ Is he willing to swim one hundred to 150 yards for a water-mark? Will he hunt in the water for a mark? Will he enthusiastically reenter the water on a double retrieve?

▼ Is he willing to penetrate rough terrain or cover and swim in stick ponds and lily pads?

▼ Will he hold his line on two-hundred-yard crosswind retrieves?

▼ Does he remember the area of the fall on marked retrieves and go to the area and hunt there with enthusiasm?

▼ If you have taught him to handle, will he willingly sit on a whistle and take casts? Will he cast into the wind and the water?

▼ On blinds, is he willing to look out from your side and take a line for one hundred or more yards or does he continually bug (look away or up at you)?

If your dog does not pass the above requirements, you can do one of two things. Either you can continue to train and run him to his maximum level, which may be a WCX, Senior Hunter degree or NAHRA Started or Intermediate title, or you can retire him from field performance events and search for another pup in hopes of obtaining one with stronger inherited field instincts.

There is nothing wrong with admitting that your dog cannot do advanced fieldwork. Don't make excuses for your dog. Accept him for what he is—a wonderful house pet, couch potato, or baby sitter, or a great therapy dog, a terrific obedience competitor, or an agility dog. Be realistic in your evaluation. It will save you many hours of anxiety and frustration.

Hunting With a Golden Retriever

Doug and Judy Spink

Doug and Judy Spink have been involved with golden retrievers for many years. They have been active in conformation, obedience, field trials, and hunt tests. They have bred and/or owned numerous champions, obedience trial champions, qualified all-age, and Master Hunter Goldens. Upon their marriage in 1994, they founded Timberline Retrievers, located in Oregon.

Timberline is a true multipurpose kennel, with both Doug and Judy strongly supporting the essential elements of the breed. Whether their puppies are competition prospects or simply cherished family companions, the focus of Timberline Retrievers is on producing dogs that are temperamentally and physically sound. Both Doug and Judy are proud to work in partnership with this truly noble breed.

It would probably be accurate to say that the majority of golden owners never have and never will actually hunt over their retrievers. This is only natural, as the breed has in a sense evolved beyond the functional role of retriever of downed game into a more robust position of family companion.

Still, many of the traits that all golden owners, hunters and non-hunters alike, find most compelling in the breed trace back directly to their heritage as hunting companions. The type of hunting for which the golden was developed and the style in which goldens were expected to hunt were perhaps the defining forces in determining the eventual outcome of the breed's development. With this in mind, I will give a brief sketch of the two main types of hunting that are done with goldens: upland and waterfowl.

Hunting Waterfowl

Everyone knows goldens are "retrievers," but what exactly is it that they are expected to retrieve? One type of hunting involves any type of waterfowl, usually migratory, from the smallest wood duck to the largest Canadian goose. Waterfowl hunting as a category has several defining characteristics. First, the waterfowl hunter almost always waits for the birds to come to her, rather than actively pursing birds. Thus, a duck hunter will spend many hours laying out a "spread" of decoys to draw the birds into shooting range. This gives waterfowl hunting a very unique "hurry up and wait" feel; once all preparations are done, the hunters wait for birds to arrive, perhaps using a duck call or other device in a attempt to hasten the process.

The Waiting Game

Of course, the retriever partakes in this waiting, as well, which is quite significant. After arriving at a site well before dawn on a chilly, stormy fall morning and setting out decoys, both hunter and dog may wait for hours in the cold before ever seeing a duck. A quality hunting dog will wait patiently but attentively for birds to arrive and will not move prematurely and risk scaring away the birds before a shot has been fired. Clearly, a dog that is unruly, whines, or insists on pacing around a small duck boat or stationary blind could be a real liability. Actually,

"Early Morning Workout"
Ch. Birnam Wood's Aarkvark N' No Play,
JH and friend Pluis Davern

Photo: Ginger Garrett

several hours spent in a twelve-foot boat with two hunting partners and an unruly dog can be taxing on even the most patient human psyche!

Mark!

During the wait, we have in the ideal golden, a calm yet attentive companion. When the birds arrive, there is a flurry of activity as the hunters choose their birds and rise in the boat to fire. With luck, there may be several birds put down in the initial volley. The retriever, during this period, is expected to "mark" each bird down. However, he must not jump out of the boat wildly after the closest fallen bird, for there may be more birds coming in, or one of the downed birds may only be injured and thus should be picked up first. This is why English hunters desired a "nonslip" retriever that would not retrieve until instructed and why our dogs are now asked to be unwaveringly "steady" at field trials.

Fetch It!

When the coast is clear, the retriever is sent for the birds and, in the case of a wounded bird, may be instructed to pick up one downed bird, in particular, before the others. At this point, the retriever's instincts may also play a key role. Any hunter can tell stories about how her dog knew that one bird was a cripple and thus the dog sought to retrieve it first, even when the hunter did not know this. One at a time, the retriever brings the birds back to the boat in a process that may take over an hour to complete if the birds have fallen in heavy cover or have traveled a fair distance after being shot. While retrieving these initial birds, the dog may watch as more birds come in and are put down, requiring the retriever to mark these birds, in addition to those that had earlier fallen.

Given these demanding requirements, it is easier to see why field breeders value the type of highly developed marking skills called for in field trials. Long water quads may seem "unnatural" at first, but while hunting waterfowl, even more challenging setups may result from a flurry of shooting and high winds or rapid currents in the water. The retriever must walk a fine line between the instinctive skills required to mark and find birds and the trainability to work with his handler to maximize the hunt. This is the essence of the golden: the fine balance between self-confidence and partnership that sets the breed apart from all others.

Blind Retrieve

Perhaps the most challenging situation in waterfowl hunting occurs when a bird is put down but, for one reason or another, the dog cannot see where it has fallen. This is the origin of blind retrieving tests, where a dog is handled to an unseen fall. Real-world water blinds in waterfowl hunting situations may be more challenging than any Open all-age test. With high winds, poor visibility of the handler, fast currents in the water, and possibly heavy cover to navigate, the tenacity and trainability of the retriever are severely tested. Of course, all this takes place in water that varies from chilly to choked with ice, and one can see how much "backbone" and force of will are required of a retriever that is to master water blinds in hunting situations.

Upland Hunting

Upland hunting, in contrast, is simpler than waterfowl hunting. In the place of boats and blinds and complex mechanics involving swamps, bogs, and rivers, the accoutrements of upland hunting are rather streamlined: a dog, a hunter, a shotgun, and (hopefully) birds in the field. While some forms of upland hunting take place from horseback, these approaches generally involve the use of pointers, rather than nonslip retrievers. Retrievers are used in upland hunting for the sportsman who approaches his quarry on foot with his dog by his side. In actuality, a good upland bird dog (be he retriever or pointer) is not exactly at the hunter's side, but rather off in the fields seeking out birds.

Upland Game Birds

Quarry for the upland hunter can run the gamut from bobwhite quail and chukar to imported pheasants (which are not native to North America, having originated in Asia) and even, in some cases, waterfowl. Of course, the type of bird being hunted is generally determined by what area of the country one calls home; quail are the purview primarily of the South, while mountain chukar are Western natives.

Hunt 'Em Up

Irrespective of the type of bird, upland hunting is about movement. The birds, for the most part, are content to lie still in the heavier sections of brush—their evolutionary heritage tells them that good camouflage and deep cover are safer than attempts to flee. While it is not unknown for a cock pheasant to be a "runner" and thus add even more aerobic excitement to an upland hunt, for the most part the birds are relatively stationary, and the hunter/retriever partnership carries the task of seeking out and flushing the game. It is this paced movement that endears the upland experience to so many; while duck hunting is often a test of perseverance in the face of long waits in very cold blinds or boats, an upland hunt can take the participants across many miles of beautiful, mountainous, memorable terrain in search of birds.

The retriever, in this game, is asked to "stay close" while he seeks out and, eventually, flushes game birds for the hunter to target. A dog who ranges too far ahead of the hunter and thus flushes birds out of shotgun range is worse than useless—he is actually spoiling the grounds for the day and is thus a frustrating companion, indeed. A measured, judicious hunt pattern on the part of a good upland dog is of paramount importance for a successful and enjoyable hunt. It is in this regard that goldens often excel.

Generally blessed with a good inborn sense of how to work a field carefully and efficiently, a good hunting golden doesn't have the reckless energy of some pointing—and even retrieving—breeds. He cues naturally off of his hunting partner, looking to his human companion for guidance and subtle suggestions on where and how to seek out game. Less a type of trained response along the lines of structured, blind retrieves, this free-form working of a field is a natural interaction between man and golden. A tip of the head, a small movement of the gun towards a section of denser brush—these are the cues that a keen golden looks for in search of well-concealed game.

When game is located, the retriever seeks to flush it. Pointers, in contrast, freeze when they get close to their quarry and wait for the hunter himself to flush the birds. The golden will stalk his quarry into the deep brush, eventually getting close enough to trigger the bird's flight response. When this happens, look out!

There are few hunting experiences as memorable—and as exciting—as having a covey of hidden quail or grouse break from cover mere yards ahead of hunter and dog. With an explosive storm of beating wings and noise, the birds are up and off.

Some types of birds, once flushed, can exceed speeds of forty miles per hour as they fly towards safety. Most upland birds stay low to the ground cover in flight and generally scatter if found in groups. The well-seasoned golden watches carefully as the birds scatter, waiting for his human partner to select and, hopefully, take down one bird (or two, if his aim is good using an over-and-under shotgun). The golden must mark where these birds fall, often in dense underbrush, which makes vision spotty.

Good Manners on the Line

The dog that simply bolts off towards whatever bird has caught his eye is a distraction at best; he may well be chasing a bird that the hunter has not targeted and could easily become lost in the thick underbrush seeking out nonexistent downed game. In contrast, the well-trained upland golden will sit while shots are fired and then await the next command after marking (to the best of his ability) downed birds.

Sent to his quarry as one would a land blind, the golden is off for his retrieval either as a traditional "marked" fall, or as a blind if the dog was unable to see the fall. In any case, a close working partnership between dog and hunter is essential to a smooth and efficient process of retrieval. Too, it is not uncommon for upland hunting to take place in mixed boggy and dry ground, necessitating good water blind skills on the part of the retriever.

In contrast to waterfowl hunting, most upland hunting involves a more subtle interaction between man and golden. While the hard-charging, cold-immune Labrador or Chesapeake might excel in some waterfowl situations, the finely tuned relationship between a golden and his human partner is often just the ticket for a wonderful day of upland hunting. It takes cleverness, teamwork, and good planning to succeed in upland hunting, and goldens often exhibit all three traits in good measure.

The golden's highly attuned nose is a real asset when seeking out the harder-to-discern scents of most upland birds. This author has seen his own goldens wind pheasants (not the most heavily-scented birds) from one hundred yards downwind, without hesitation. This sort of laser-effective nose makes finding well-hidden upland quarry an achievable target.

The "Perfect Day"

Upland hunting brings with it many special moments, and most golden owners who enjoy this form of sport are well aware of the deep bond that naturally develops in these situations. A well-seasoned team of golden and partner working the bright, crisp fall fields in search of elusive quarry makes a beautiful sight. Nary a word is spoken or a sound made as dog and man or woman systematically work their way through the terrain, keying off one another's strengths—in man, his knowledge of bird behavior and patterns; in dog, his unbelievably good nose and instinctive ability to second-guess good hiding spots for quarry. Then, in a flash, a bird will explode from hiding. The shotgun sounds, a word is spoken to golden, and a beautiful addition to the dinner table is soon in hand.

If waterfowl hunting rewards tenacity, patience, and careful planning, then upland hunting with a retriever is enlivened by good instincts, a dog who enjoys working in partnership with his owner, and fast reflexes on the part of man and dog. Most breeds tend to excel at one or another; golden retrievers excel at both.

The Ideal Hunting Dog

The ideal hunting dog is alert yet calm, steady yet keen, self-confident yet tractable, and instinctive yet trainable. Of course, this description fits the golden perfectly and is at the core of the entire breed standard. After all, the golden was developed to fulfill a functional role, not to match a physical "breed standard." Only after the functional elements had been defined was the breed standard written and adopted by golden breeders. Without its hunting heritage, and without a continuing presence in hunting situations, the golden could be cast loose from its original purpose, its genetic makeup defined more by how it should look (the standard) than what it should do and how it should behave.

Search and Rescue

Kathryn L. Jones

Kathryn L. Jones was born into the care of a working curly-coated retriever. Growing up, her family owned both All-American crosses and AKC-registered companions. As an adult, Kate didn't own a golden, but her father did. Upon his death, his beloved golden retriever bitch went to live with Kate and thus began her introduction to the breed.

Circa 1990, when the plentiful natural disasters of California prompted her to action, she knew she could be most effective as one-half of a canine search and rescue team. After waiting more or less patiently for her old girl to live to an undisturbed old age, she adopted a one-year-old male through Northern California Golden Retriever Rescue. He completed his initial area search and rescue training, but was unable to pass the final certification tests because of elbow dysplasia. She ultimately found her current partner, Goodtimes Free's Company (Crissy) through the kind help of Janis Teichman and the generosity of Sylvia Donahey, Maryle Malloy, and Marie Deyl, her co-owners. Wilderness area searches are their focus.

To improve their search skills, Kate and Crissy have traveled around California and Nevada. They have walked in parades, visited the Mark Hopkins Hotel in San Francisco (to learn about revolving doors and staff a safety fair), taken excursions in helicopters, and trained on agility equipment.

Kate holds a law degree and is a professional mediator. She and her goldens live on a couple of acres just outside San Jose, California. Kate is a member of California Rescue Dog Association, Palo Alto Foothills Tracking Association, and Santa Clara Dog Training Club. She has helped with tracking tests as tracklayer, cross-track layer, chief tracklayer, and secretary. She is a recovering horse addict who enjoys reading mysteries. Kate never seriously considered any breed but a golden for the job as her search and rescue partner.

The Golden Retriever In Search and Rescue

Search and Rescue Qualities

Golden retrievers are part of search and rescue because goldens have significant natural talents needed for the job. These talents result from decades of thoughtful breeding for a good hunting companion. They include a powerful hunting drive, strong human orientation, good nose, suitable color, appropriate physical characteristics, and sound mind.

A strong hunting drive because a search assignment can last as long as twelve continuous hours in a day working each day for a full week. You may work all day and find nothing because there is nothing to find. While most assignments are in the two- to eight-hour range, the team must be able to work extended hours when needed. Part of a handler's job is to protect the golden from its own drive, calling the dog in to lie down, get a drink, and rest on a regular schedule. The rest period frequency and length varies with the type of search and the weather.

Denise Corliss and her Golden Retriever responding to the World Trade Center disaster. Deployed to "ground zero" with the Texas Task Force 1.

Photo Credit: TX-TF1

Left: Crissy "up" in harness (notice her smile!)

Below: Kate and Crissy (Goodtimes Free's Company) helicopter training

A golden's love of people offers several benefits in search and rescue. A dog that searches for people will be more motivated if the dog likes people. It will also respond more quickly to training as it works to please its handler. Goldens also benefit from some of the most talented positive advertising in the world, thanks to various movies. This means a large part of the public welcomes the golden search dog in searches, training, and public events.

The golden nose that searches for people owes a special debt of gratitude to the bloodhound that went into the mix of creating the breed. People are found buried in snow, rubble, dirt, sand, and mud, on cliffs, up in trees, in ditches and drains, and wormed into the thickest thickets. This creates a variety of problems in pinpointing the scent source. A sensitive nose helps. The handler has the responsibility of educating the dog's nose by incrementally increasing the difficulty of the scent problems so that the dog is able to solve difficult location problems, but the final call belongs to the golden.

The physical appearance of a golden is helpful in search and rescue in several ways. The breed's moderate size provides a golden with an ability to cover ground and obstacles, but is still small enough for them to be lifted into helicopters. The color of the golden helps, too, but not for camouflage or aesthetic reasons. Experience has shown that people unfamiliar with dogs are more accepting of light-colored dogs. Even people who fear dogs are usually more comfortable with a well-mannered golden than a darker-colored dog of equally good manners.

Every search golden must be physically sound to the point of sturdiness. The search golden will train and work hard its whole life, jumping and moving on all kinds of footing. A search and rescue golden becomes more valuable as it matures and accumulates experience. While senses may start to fade at ten or twelve years, until then the mature dog is sought after as the "experienced one." You may have wondered why you rarely see search goldens in regular training trials. It is not snobbery; it is protection. By training for search and rescue, I have accepted an obligation. If my golden is going to be injured, it should happen on a search. I am not willing to risk my partner's service value on anything else. For example, my current partner badly sprained a paw jumping up for a ball in her reward play. Veterinary, chiropractor, and acupuncture treatments notwithstanding, I am lucky she recovered. Now her ball is rolled, not thrown, and her "boulders into the creek" agility play has ended.

Last but not least **the golden's famous even-tempered character** rates in my mind as one of its strongest values in the search and rescue world. The search golden is expected to ignore the most obnoxious, distracting, and ridiculous things in the world. Sirens, unstable footing, emergency power generators, running rabbits and deer, helicopter landings, water fowl, all-terrain vehicle rides, shared open truck beds down a bad dirt road, busy freeways ten feet away, irrational people, and traversing thin air by harness, rope, and pulley all challenge them while their nice comfy crate is miles away. Support teams relax because the golden is next in line. They know the golden will handle it with the cool of a professional.

Search and Rescue Defined

Not every golden can or should be a search dog. How do you pick out the search golden? One preliminary is to know what type of search work can be done. While many of the same qualities are needed in any search dog, different specialties emphasize different strengths. Although the National Association for Search and Rescue has guidelines and evaluations, search and rescue in the United States is typically organized at the county level. There is no national certification requirement for search dogs outside the federal urban search and rescue teams that deploy under the Federal Emergency Management Agency (FEMA).

But most search goldens are not trained for urban disaster. They are trained for trailing, area, cadaver, evidence, water, avalanche, and even fire. Trailing is a close cousin to tracking, where many goldens achieve multiple certifications. Area search dogs rely on the quartering tactics of a good hunting dog as their handler covers the geographic area assigned to the team. Cadaver goldens hone their scent-source skills down to inches, identifying visually indistinguishable remains from the surroundings. Evidence dogs extend the object of their search to include items (branches, personal property, even soil) touched by the search subject. Both cadaver and evidence goldens must overcome the golden's natural tendency to pick up the find. The team must avoid disturbing other possible evidence. The water search for drowning victims seems a natural for water-loving goldens, but, in fact, most water searches are done from boats and at the water line. A canine-assisted water search increases the chance of recovery, decreases search time (especially in murky water), and, in hazardous waters, decreases the risk to divers. Goldens, with their warm double coat, find avalanche work invigorating, but handlers trade off being buried deep in the snow for each other in training. Avalanche rescue requires that the team be nearby as an uninjured, buried avalanche victim will suffocate in a few hours' time. After a fire, it may not be known whether there were any human victims. A fire-trained canine cadaver team can speed the answer to that question with reliability. While a good search golden will search out what it is trained to find, the handler must have the fortitude to keep the dog motivated even when the handler is affected by the condition of the subject when found. This is often the case in fire and cadaver searches, and this reality plays a role in every branch of search and rescue.

Some of these specialties have a complimentary overlap; others are traditionally kept separate. An area or a trailing search dog may encounter a dead or drowned subject and the team will train to deal with this sad end to a search. Avalanche goldens may be trailing or area dogs in other situations, but a trailing dog is generally not cross-trained as an area dog, or vice versa. This is not a reflection of canine ability. It is a matter of evidence clarity in legal proceedings, should they arise. At some sites a golden that normally works off lead will be worked on lead for its safety. For example, an area or cadaver dog working along an unfenced road, near a collapsing surface, or close to poison bait stations might be expected to work on lead.

Separate from civilian search and rescue teams, a distinct branch of highly trained law enforcement canines exists. These are rarely goldens. These dogs may be trained for police work (including weapon detection, drug smuggling, and suspect apprehension), agricultural imports (any crop not processed through U.S. agricultural import procedures and illegal imports), or arson detection. The arson detection dog and the search dog trained for fire serve different purposes. The arson dog locates evidence of arson. The fire-trained cadaver dog locates the remains of those killed by fire.

Choosing a Golden Retriever for Search and Rescue

First you must accept the fact that the best partner (dog) is one who will persist when it has workable scent, even though you try to call it off. If you are looking at a litter, be sure to ask which pup is the escape artist, the one the breeder is most concerned about placing successfully. Take a long look at that one. It has the creativity to figure out scent source location problems. Which pups are bold and friendly? Which play the longest? Identify the pups with the best bone structure and tight, balanced paws. If you plan on neutering your pup, you are free to focus on your needs as a searcher. If you may breed your partner, you will need to take many more factors into consideration.

You can also find a good search partner without the risks and extra time required with a pup. Many experienced searchers prefer to find a youngster to train. You can see your partner's adult form. You have a better chance of avoiding structural weakness. With patience you can find a dog that already has some of the training basics in place, such as obedience, field trial, tracking, or agility. How does such a prize become available? The same way most rescued goldens find themselves looking for a new home—a change in family commitments, illness or death of the owner, a dog that is just "too much" for its original family, or a dog that won't be bred "after all."

Why Search and Rescue?

The idea of working a golden that contributes to the community attracts you. You can train personal service pups, qualify your dog for therapy work, or train both yourself and your golden for search and rescue work. Each is a wonderful contribution. If television appearances, renown, and glamour attract you, do not choose search and rescue. If you like sliding down muddy hillsides through poison oak on your vacation time, crawling through collapsed, stinking structures, finding stinging nettle through personal contact, training and working in blinding dust or driving rain, lying buried under a pile of rubble for the day while others train and test with their dogs, or living with ticks as fellow searchers, you may be a good candidate for search and rescue work. Although some families do point out that counseling is cheaper.

What motivates the golden owner to search and rescue work? How does one come to devote virtually all one's time, one's precious partner, nights of sleep, and much money to lousy working conditions with no pay? The searcher's reasons are as individual as the searcher. For some, it is an outgrowth of professional skills. Firefighters, police, military personnel, park rangers, search divers, and other security personnel may see the value of a trained canine partner in their work. For the owner with a history of multi-talented champion performers, it may offer the chance to work one golden all its life in a field where the dog's increasing skill is not only admired but used. For some, it is the path to the satisfaction of taking action when disaster strikes.

A Search and Rescue Lifestyle

What is the typical schedule of a student search dog handler with a standard work week? With your golden, obedience class one night, agility or field training another day, and search skill training at least twice each week. You train with your partner so that you understand his or her body language so well that you recognize what your golden is scenting even when you are tired or distracted or without light. You will ensure your partner knows how to swim. A storm will not cancel training. The most urgent searches are conducted during storms. The chance to train in a storm is a valuable opportunity to check both your performance and hone your partner's practical working skills. If the team is fortunate enough to live in an area with an active search dog organization, the handler may rearrange the "other" job to suit his or her search training. After initial qualification, regular requalification is often required. Training never stops as you develop new specialties and hone existing skills.

You will also spend time learning your own search team skills—your half of the team obligations. Typical handler skills include obtaining and maintaining advanced first aid certification, radio use qualifications, professional CPR certification, physical fitness qualification, appropriate survival skills, demonstration of knowledge of scent behavior as affected by terrain, buildings, time, and weather, interview skills, developing a search plan appropriate for the assignment, and showing map and compass skills in several formats. Training is ongoing as new tools and methods develop. Some skills require regular recertification.

The handler must also have ready assistance available at home. Only the search dog responds with the handler. There is no accommodation for other dogs at a search. If single, the searcher must have prior arrangements for someone to tend animals at home or limit the team's response to short local searches. If the searcher lives with family, family support, or at least cooperation, is needed. This is complicated by the fact that many search call-outs occur in the middle of the night. Holidays are another common time for searches as that is when many people travel to unfamiliar locations.

Living with a search golden is different than living with a competition dog in some ways. Mistakes at home in play or lifestyle set back your personal competition goals. Those same mistakes at home may cost someone's life with a search golden. Your partner is taking too long finding the ball and you need to go? How do you explain to your hard-working partner that this scent source is not as important as the one on a search? Tempted to scold it for insisting? How will you revive that insistence when you are out searching? Play with your dog is circumscribed by behaviors you need in the search; if your partner is ball obsessed, you may need to restrict it as only a reward for a find. My point is that training a search golden is not limited to a daily training session. Search training is an integral part of living with your partner. You ignore the impact of your routine interactions with your golden at the risk of impairing your partner's performance during a search.

Social Obligations

You may also encounter criticism from strangers. A respectful, courteous, and educational answer is the only acceptable response. This is true whenever you are identified as part of a canine search team, by word, behavior, or uniform. You and your dog may be the only search team this person ever meets. Search teams need public cooperation and support. It is your behavior and your dog's that will determine this stranger's future comments and attitude to searchers. So be ready to explain your "skinny" dog, why your dog is off lead or in a no-dog area, or any of many other unusual situations your training and work may create.

The golden in public service has "social" obligations as well as working commitments. In a quest for education, the public reaches out to search dogs. Public, school, and corporate safety fairs invite search dogs (and their handlers) to present information on how the search dog works, how to avoid getting lost, and what to do if lost. At a fair, the information table with the most interesting, professional presentation draws the most attention. While search goldens are a wonderful draw themselves, they and their handlers also work to create an attractive presentation. The dog may learn fun "parlor" tricks, and the handler bathes and brushes and trims the dog to eliminate any hint of the dirt and stickers they searched through a few days ago. When meeting the public, the handler knows an important percentage of people are not enamored of dogs. The search golden that jumps on people does not belong at a presentation to the general public. The presenting golden also needs good oral hygiene. "Dog breath" or bad teeth simply do not make the grade.

Federal Emergency Management Agency—FEMA Urban Disaster—Oklahoma City

One of my earliest SAR trainings occurred shortly after the Oklahoma City bombing. The FEMA team from my home state (California) had returned from that disaster no more than forty-eight hours earlier. Visibly tired, they gave a clear report of their experiences and the successes achieved based on their "beyond expectations" level of training. The handlers stated plainly that the Oklahoma bomb site had features different from sites created by natural disasters.

The Oklahoma City bombing was dreadful, but in comparison to the sixteen acres of devastation at the World Trade Center, it was small. As I write this, less than a year has passed since the 9/11 terrorist attacks. I struggle to find words. But images come to me, images of goldens eager to get to work, stubbornly working to locate someone, anyone, reminding their human half that their canine nose is the reason for the team. The human searches declare an area clear; the dog says otherwise. And later, another fallen hero recovered—just as the dog said it would be. Search dogs don't read floor plans or discuss probabilities. They use facts, established by old-fashioned nose work. They also do double duty, offering on-the-scene stress relief to other searchers.

The World Trade Center—September 11, 2001

The United States now has about one hundred FEMA-qualified dogs. This is about one-third of the desired number of canine teams. All FEMA teams, with their healthy canine team members, were rotated in to search the September 11 sites. No matter how skilled, a sick or injured dog does not qualify to respond to a disaster call-out. No FEMA-qualified search dog suffered serious injury at the World Trade Center. That is a purpose of the difficult qualification tests. Newspapers reported that three hundred dogs searched at the World Trade Center. In the first hours after a disaster, owners volunteer dogs not qualified for urban disaster. These dogs and their owners are at high risk of injury. I believe

Riley at the World Trade Center
Photo: Journalist 1st Class Preston Keres, U.S. Navy, U.S. Navy photo courtesy of
McDonnell-Douglas

He is fifty feet up in a canyon of WTC wreckage. He is on his way out after the stan-
dard twelve-hour shift. Just before Riley, the line and basket were used to remove the
body of a New York firefighter.

Riley is suspended by two systems from the high line. The orange "vest" is a lifting
harness that connects to the high line independently of the open Stokes basket (a spe-
cialized form of rescuer's stretcher) in which Riley is lying. Both the harness and the
Stokes are connected to the high line by a separate set of travelers (the "wheel" items
above the line).

the report of three hundred dogs at the World Trade Center stems
from an assumption that the desired number of FEMA-qualified
search dogs was the actual number of qualified dogs com-
pounded by the normal confusion following a major disaster and
the presence of nonqualified dog handlers trying to help.

The FEMA-qualified dogs are valued by other task force
members as well as frightened families of victims. On their flight
home, search and rescue dogs CA-TF3 and NV-TK1 shared a
commercial liner drawn into military service. On each side of the
aisle were three seats. After their hard work, the canine team
members were delighted to stretch out on a nice soft bed of seats.
Even though it meant some nonhandlers had to share a row of

seats with a dog, they let the sleeping dogs lie. Another task force realized on its flight home that the dogs needed to be removed from the cold floor of their uninsulated military plane. Even though some dogs ended up in their handlers' laps for the balance of the trip, the team made sure the dogs were kept warm.

Golden Retriever Heroes at the World Trade Center

Of the nearly one hundred FEMA-qualified canine search teams, I have been able to identify the following goldens who searched the World Trade Center site with their handlers:

▼ Ana, a rescued golden—National Disaster Search Dog Foundation, with Fire Capt. Rick Lee; CA-TF7

▼ Dausen V.D. Nuinivand (Dausen, imported from Switzerland) who also worked Oklahoma City, with Sharon Gattas; CA-TF6

▼ Dusty, a rescued golden—National Disaster Search Dog Foundation, with Fire Capt. Randy Gross; CA-TF7

▼ Emberain Orion the Hunter (Orion) with Bob Macaulay, who also worked Oklahoma City with DeeDee's Quasar Goldenlight (Quasar); CA-TF4

▼ Harley with Battalion Chief Rob Cima—Eldorado County FD; CA-TF7

▼ Huggybears Radar O Riley (Riley) with Fire Capt. Chris Selfridge—Johnstown Fire Dept.; PA-TF1

▼ Louie with Amy Rising; NE-TF1

▼ The Beauty of Bretagne (Bretagne) with Denise F. Corliss; TX-TF1

▼ Thunder with Kent Olson; WA-TF1

▼ Woody with Fire Lt. Terry Trepanier—Washington Township FD; OHTF1

I thank each of these handlers for their efforts at the World Trade Center and at other searches and for their efforts to become and remain qualified for urban disaster searches.

I thank Lynne J. Englebert, Section Chief of Training, NASA Ames Disaster Assistance & Rescue Team, CA-TF4, and Rue Chagoll, author of "Goldens at Ground Zero," *Golden Retriever News* for their help in gathering information on urban disasters and the World Trade Center search effort. Any inaccuracies are mine.

Retirement

There is a final piece to the pattern that makes up the life of a golden search dog. If you are lucky, you will train and work with one golden for ten years. You will be so close, your spouse and children may be a bit envious. You know the time is coming for him to retire, as much for his safety as for your effectiveness on a search. You will get a new pup to start training. Your experienced partner will give it some pointers. Somehow, you start giving your trust to the newcomer. You must, to do the job. Maybe you will give your partner a dignified end; maybe he will leave on his own schedule. But he will remain in your heart and mind during every search for the rest of your life, reminding you of all he taught you. The hardest part is living up to his image of you, because he always thought you were as good as he was. A golden is a tough act to follow.

Appendix

▼ Suggested Reading: Magazines and Books
▼ Videos and CDs
▼ Clubs and Organizations
▼ Web Sites
▼ Equipment and Supplies
▼ Bibliography

"The Head-Start program" – Author's granddaughter Jessica Eichner

Suggested Reading

Magazines

The Golden Retriever News

The definitive magazine for the breed

The Golden Retriever News is published bimonthly by the Golden Retriever Club of America, Inc. (GRCA) in order to help promote and protect the interests of the breed in all areas, as well as to serve as a means of communication and source of information to breeders and owners. The GRNews is sent only to GRCA members. Complete the Membership Application (included in the Appendix) to join the GRCA and receive the magazine.

Front and Finish

H & S Publications, Inc., P.O. Box 333, Galesburg, IL 61601. Covers all aspects of obedience training and competition.

AKC Gazette

The American Kennel Club, 51 Madison Avenue, New York, NY 10010. Published monthly by the American Kennel Club. The Gazette carries all official information on AKC business, rules changes, etc. as well as excellent general articles and national breed columns. An "Awards" supplement listing all new AKC titles and AKC event results is also available.

Gun Dog

P.O. Box 343, Mt. Morris, IL 61054. Articles on training and hunting for the various gun dog breeds, including goldens.

Clean Run

35 Walnut St., Turner Falls, MA 01376. The magazine for dog agility trainers and enthusiasts.

Golden Retriever Weekly—Online Magazine

www.grweekly.com/

Books

Golden Retrievers

Bauer, Nona Kilgore. *The World of the Golden Retriever*. TFH, 1993.

Cairns, Julie. *The Golden Retriever; An Owner's Guide To A Happy, Healthy Pet*. Howell, 1995.

Fisher, Gertrude. *The New Complete Golden Retriever*. 2nd ed. Howell, 1984.

Schlehr, Marcia. *The New Golden Retriever*. Howell, 1996.

Training and Care
Benjamin, Carol. *Mother Knows Best; The Natural Way To Train Your Dog.* Howell, 1985.

Monks of New Skete. *How To Be Your Dog's Best Friend.* Little, Brown, 1978.

Rutherford, Clarice and David Neil. *How To Raise A Puppy You Can Live With.* 2nd ed. Alpine, 1992.

Vollmer, Peter. *Super Puppy; How To Raise The Best Dog You'll Ever Have!* 2nd ed. Super Puppy Press, 1988.

Behavior and Psychology
Fox, Michael W. Superdog; *Raising The Perfect Canine Companion.* Howell, 1996.

Fox, Michael W. *Understanding Your Dog.* St. Martin, 1992.

Pryor, Karen. *Don't Shoot The Dog; The New Art of Teaching and Training.* Bantam, 1985.

Conformation Showing
Alston, George and Connie Vanacore. *The Winning Edge; Showring Secrets.* Howell, 1992.

Vanacore, Connie. *Dog Showing; An Owner's Guide.* Howell, 1990.

Obedience, Agility and Tracking
Bauman, Diane L. *Beyond Basic Dog Training.* 2nd ed. Howell, 1991.

Burnham, Patricia Gail. *Play Training Your Dog.* St. Martin's, 1985.

Johnson, Glen R. *Tracking Dog; Theory And Methods.* Amer., 1975.

Pearsall, Milo D. and Hugo Verbruggen. *Scent: Training To Track, Search And Rescue.* Alpine, 1982.

Simmons-Moake, Jane. *Agility Training; The Fun Sport For All Dogs.* Howell, 1992.

Health
Carlson, Delbert G. and James M. Giffen. *Dog Owners Home Veterinary Guide.* 2nd ed. Howell, 1992.

Structure and Movement
Elliott, Rachel Page. *The New Dogsteps.* 2nd ed. Howell, 1983.

Schlehr, Marcia. *A Study Of The Golden Retriever.* 3rd ed. Travis House, 1994.

Breeding

Craige, Patricia V. *Born To Win: Breed To Succeed*. Doral, 1997.

Holst, Phyllis A. *Canine Reproduction; A Breeder's Guide.* Alpine, 1987.

Walkowicz, Chris and Bonnie Wilcox. *Successful Dog Breeding*. 2nd ed. Howell, 1994.

Field

Dobbs, Jim and Phyllis Dobbs. *Tri-Tronics Retriever Training*. Tri-Tronics, Inc., 1993.

Rutherford, Clarice and Cherylon Loveland. *Retriever Puppy Training; The Right Start For Hunting*. Alpine, 1988.

Spencer, James B. *Retriever Training Tests*. 2nd ed. Alpine, 1997.

Videos and CDs

The Golden Retriever by Rachel Page Elliott for the Golden Retriever Club of America, 31 minutes. U.S. and Canada, $20 plus $4.50 shipping. Overseas, $20 plus $10 shipping. Order from Debbie Ascher, P.O. Box 69, Berthoud, CO 80513. Make checks payable to GRCA.

Sirius Puppy Training by Dr. Ian Dunbar, 90 minutes. $19.95 plus $4.95 postage and handling. Order from Resolution Video, P.O. Box 2284, S. Burlington, VT 05407. (800) 862-8900.

Grooming Your Golden by Delaware Valley Golden Retriever Rescue. $24.95. Send order to Delaware Valley Golden Retriever Rescue, Attn: Video Order, P.O. Box 2321, Sinking Springs, PA 19608-0321.

DOG STEPS—A Study of Canine Structure and Movement by Rachel Page Elliott, 1 hour and 9 minutes. $49.95. Write to them for current ordering information: The American Kennel Club, Attn: Videos, 51 Madison Avenue, New York, NY 10010. To place credit card orders by phone call (212) 696-8392.

Sound Beginnings Retriever Training by Jackie Mertens. A Comprehensive and progressive training program for retriever puppies from 7 weeks to 8 months of age. It can also be used to introduce an adult retriever to the world of retrieving. $39.95, Available from Younglove Broadcast Services, Inc., P.O. Box 79, Metamora, MI 48455-0079, (800) 595-7965 [Outside U.S. (810) 678-2313] webmaster@ybsmedia.com.

Dogs Are Problem Solvers: Complete Obedience Training: The Connie Cleveland Method. The Connie Cleveland Method shows you the steps necessary to train your dog for obedience (from basic commands to utility exercises). This method focuses on how dogs learn, why dogs make mistakes, and how to respond to your dog's errors and correct performance. The program also shows you what skills can be taught concurrently. Includes 3 VHS videotapes, a comprehensive manual and a set of skill charts. $129.99 USD. Available from Younglove Broadcast Services, Inc., P.O. Box 79, Metamora, MI 48455-0079, (800) 595-7965 [Outside U.S. (810) 678-2313] webmaster@ybsmedia.com

Interactive – CD The Golden Retriever. Complete Multimedia Guide Of The Golden Retriever. $39.95 (US) plus shipping. To order E-Mail or www.k9cd.com. Call (800) 662-4118 or (253) 631-1442.

Clubs and Organizations

The Golden Retriever Club of America, Inc. (GRCA)
c/o Secretary, P.O. Box 20434
Oklahoma City, OK 73156
National information line (281) 861-0820.
Web site: www.grca.org

American Kennel Club, Inc. (AKC)
51 Madison Avenue
New York, NY 10010
Telephone: (212) 696-8200
Web site: www.akc.org

Customer Service & Registrations
5580 Centerview Drive
Raleigh, NC 27606
Telephone: (919) 233-9767

Rules and Regulations for Events
The American Kennel Club Order Desk
5580 Centerview Drive
Raleigh, NC 27606-3390
Tel: (919) 233-9767
Email: orderdesk@akc.org

The AKC regulates its approved events such as dog shows, obedience trials, field trials, tracking tests and its titles, as well as all registration of purebred litters and individual dogs. For a complete list of all their services and products, visit the Web site: www.akc.org:

Canadian Kennel Club (CKC)
89 Skyway Avenue, Suite 100
Etobicoke, Ontario M9W 6R4
Phone: (800) 250-8040 or (416) 675-5511
Fax: (416) 675-6506
Email: information@ckc.com

Orthopedic Foundation For Animals (OFA)
2300 Nifong Blvd.
Columbia, MO 65201.
Information on x-raying for OFA evaluation

Pet Recovery

AKC Companion Animal Recovery
5580 Centerview Dr., Suite 250
Raleigh, NC 27606-3394.
Registry for micro chipped or tattooed animals.

North American Hunting Retriever Association (NAHRA)
P.O. Box 1590
Stafford, VA 22555
(540) 286-0625.

Information on NAHRA-sponsored hunting retriever tests. Contains a 24-hour recovery network to aid in the recovery and return of lost pets.

Synbiotics (PENNHIP Information)
Pennsylvania Hip Improvement Program
11011 Via Frontera
San Diego, CA 92127
Information on PennHip Program and the distraction method of evaluating hip laxity.

Canine Eye Registration Foundation (CERF)
1248 Lynn Hall, Purdue University
West Lafayette, IN 47907
Registration of eye examined dogs—all breeds

Web Sites of Interest

Golden Retriever Club Of America   www.grca.org

Joining a local golden retriever club is one of the best ways to participate in activities and events specifically designed to increase your knowledge and enjoyment of the breed. Opportunities abound for learning and socializing with other fanciers. It is one of the best ways to gain information and practical experience in training for hunting/field work, obedience, agility, conformation (dog shows), tracking, search and rescue and other activities in which golden retrievers excel.

Lifelong friendships are often forged between those who participate in club activities. I can testify to the fact that my life has been enriched a hundred fold by the friends and acquaintances I made while participating in club activities. It was here that I found the mentors who help guide my breeding program and who helped me teach my dogs to hunt and work in the field, to strut around the showring and earn championship titles, and to pay attention and perform basic obedience exercises not only to earn titles, but to become better companions.

The Web site lists each first by state then by name. Many of the clubs have their own Web site, which you can access through the grca.org site. The club's address is generally the Club Secretary, and that person may change from year to year.

GRCA Puppy Referral

www.grca.org

Club Web Sites

Yankee Golden Retriever Rescue   www.ygrr.org
NORCAL Golden Retriever Rescue   www.golden-rescue.org
Chesapeake Bay Retriever Rescue   www.cbrrescue.org

Supplier Web Sites

PetEdge (formerly NESerum Company)* www.PetEdge.com
    Equipment, supplies and toys for dogs, cats, birds, and small animals

    Grateful acknowledgment to this company for furnishing pictures of all supplies and equipment for this book.

www.dogsafield.com/
    Equipment and supplies for all types of field events

www.gundogsupply.com/
    Field and hunting supplies

www.jandjdog.com
    Obedience and agility equipment

www.max200.com/
    Agility and obedience equipment

www.pawsforthought.com/
    Booster Bath
    Tropical Shower

www.source-m.com/
    Great Site For Golden Goodies

www.ybsmedia.com/
  Retriever Videos, Including Connie Cleveland And Jackie Mertens

Health Web Sites

www.vet.purdue.edu/
  Purdue University

www.offa.org/
  OFA

www.vetmedcenter.com/
  Medical Information for Pet Owners

www.naturalrearing.com
  Holistic Newsletter and Health Information

Contributing Author Web Sites

Jackie Mertens   www.topbrass-retrievers.com/

Connie Cleveland   www.dogtrainersworkshop.com/

Doug and Judy Spink   www.timberlineretrievers.com

Children's Web Sites

Jan Wall's site   www.loveyourdog.com

Informative Web Sites

www.golden-retriever.com/

Golden Retrievers in Cyberspace:
Resource for information, links and Golden Retriever Rescue

www.working-retriever.com/
  Working Retriever Central

www.fieldgoldenretriever.com/
  For Field Enthusiasts

United States Dog Agility Association (USDAA)
  P. O. Box 850995
  Richardson, Texas 75085-0955
  Phone: (972) 231-9700
  Email: info@usdaa.com

Agility Association of Canada (AAC)
  RR 2
  Lucan, Ontario N0N 2J0
  Canada
  Phone: (519) 657-7636

www.everythinggolden.com/
On Line News Magazine dedicated to golden retrievers

Golden Retriever Pedigrees - Open Database
www.k9data.com

Agility Web Sites

www.agilitynet.com

www.cleanrun.com

www.dogpatch.org/agility/

Golden Retriever Art Web Sites

Dogarte: Maryle Malloy@msn.com and the web site: www.dogarte.com

"Companions" by Mia Lane, our Cover Artist. Limited Edition Print
Available
www.muttart.com

Michael Jurogue Johnson - Incredible art - Born with Down syndrome,
Michael displays an amazing sense of wonder and determination to
communicate with others.
michaelsart.landofpuregold.com/
www.art.com
www.vaughanart.com
www.animalstamps.com
www.nature-art.net
www.mydogart.com
countrysideart.com

John Weiss
www.galleryak.com/l
www.k9gifts.com/dog-statues/golden.html

Kathy Hagerman: One of my personal favorites. I own several of her
pieces.
www.kathyhagerman.com

Katie Ropar: I adore her work. Her ability to capture goldens and children
is astounding. Her "Buddies" has a place of honor in my home office.
www.shopsadesign.com/katie.html

Debi DeNardi Photography: Beautiful photography of golden retrievers
www.sherwoodgoldens.com

Kathy Partridge: Another of my favorite artists—she knows golden
retrievers!
www.partridgeart.com

Equipment and Supplies

The equipment and supplies recommended in this book may be found in many of the catalogs listed in this section. Some are available at pet stores and supermarkets, and most are available through various vendors at dog shows in both the United States and Canada.

This appendix contains the name and product number for all the products I recommend from the PetEdge catalog. Pet Edge (formerly NESerum) is the company I typically choose when ordering products and supplies. Their catalog is comprehensive and the prices competitive. When I approached them with the idea of furnishing pictures for the book, they were immediately cooperative. Although they did not request that I list the product numbers or ask for any remuneration, this is my way of saying "thank you."

PetEdge: www.PetEdge.com

For a catalog call: (800) PET-EDGE (800) 738-3343

House Training

Natures Miracle	NM11091
"Baby" Gate	NL44204
Airline Crate	D037430
Wire Crate	MW53742

Crate Training

See Above

Grooming

#1 All Systems Shampoo	AL85412
#1 All Systems Conditioner (gallon)	AL95416
#1 All Systems Slicker Brush (small)	AL100
#1 All Systems Pin Brush (large)	AL89562
Greyhound Comb (fine/course)	ZW60914
Mat Rake	ZX01001
Nail Grinder	ZW77000
Nail Clippers	TP61718
Liquid Bandage	TP45498
Challengaire 2000 Canine Dryer	DK200009
Grooming Table with Arm	GC21736
Grooming Noose	ZW100
Thinning Shears - 44/22	ZT442200
Regular Shears	TS31888

House and Yard

Pooper Scooper	ZW671
Flea Spray	FA12317
Bitter Apple Repellent	VA1181
Chain Link Dog Kennel	ZW153
Underground Fence System	
Stainless Steel Bowl	ZW69064
Stainless Steel Water Bucket	
Comfortable Dog Bed	CN400
Portable Exercise Pen	ZW12848
Smart Dog Premium Fence System	ZX931
Flat Sided Stainless Steel Water Pail	ZT544

Health Aids

Nemex Wormer	X40016
Carry All for First Aid Kit	HP58345
First Aid Kit	ZW42118
Ear Cleaner/OtiClean-A	AG10018
Ear Dry/Oti Clean -B	AG66602
Tooth Cleaning - Petrodex	SJ531

Training Aids

Nylon Adjustable Collar	TP114
Brass Name Plate for Collar	TP60029
Martingale Adjustable Collar	TP633
Collar "choke chain"	ZW330
Show Collar (18" to 22")	ZT139
Flexi Lead	FE710
Long Line	TP618
Kangaroo Leather Show Lead	ZX276
Flat Leather Leash 6'	CP669

Toys

Tennis Balls	ZW255 group
Plush toys with balls inside	ZW701
Latex Squeekie Toys	ZW752
Plush toys that talk	ZW495
Tennis Balls (2) Rope Toy	ZW80113
Plush Toys with balls and long legs	ZW923
Flippy Flyers (Nylon Frisbee)	ZT966
Kong Toy (indestructible bouncing toy)	KC15015
Nylabone Dino (great for puppy teeth)	TF22101
Sterile Bones	R10210
Absorbent Chamois Towel	ZC4010
Booster Bath Tub	ZC10055

Bibliography

Books

Fischer, Gertrude. *The New Complete Golden Retriever.* 1984. Howell Book House.

Fogle, Bruce, DVM. *Dog Breed Handbooks: The Golden Retriever.* 1999. DK Publishing.

Grossman, Alvin, Ph.D. *Winning With Pure Bred Dogs.* 1991. Doral Publishing.

Kilgore, Nonna. *Golden Retriever for Dummies.* 2000. Hungry Minds Publishing.

Palika, Liz. *How To Train Your Golden Retriever.* 1988. Howell Book House.

Pepper, Jeffrey. *The Golden Retriever.* 1985. TFH Publications.

Spira, Harry, DVM. *Canine Terminology.* 1982. Harper & Row Publishers.

Magazines

AKC Gazette
260 Madison Ave.
New York, NY 10016

Dogs in Canada
Canadian Kennel Club
89 Skyway Ave, #200
Etobicoke, Ontario, Canada M9W 6R4

Golden Retriever Review
13029 Gladstone Ave.
Sylmar, CA 91342

Index